Thai

Edited by Fred Sandman

BARNES & NOBLE

NEW YORK

contents

6 From Nature's Garden
The Most Important Ingredients

8 Step by Step
Thai Kitchen Basics

10 Snacks and Salads
From Chicken Satay with Peanut Sauce
to Rice Noodle Salad with Duck

38 Soups and Vegetables
From Coconut Milk Soup with Shrimp
to Vegetable Rice in Banana Leaf

70 Fish and Seafood
From Red Bream with Chili and Lemongrass
to Squid Rings with Thai Basil

98 Poultry and Meat
From Red Chicken Curry with Cherry Tomatoes
to Fried Noodles with Beef and Sprouts

128 Index of recipes

From Nature's Garden
The Most Important Ingredients

Thai cuisine is considered to be one of the most varied in the world. Its secret lies in the fact that it uses simple ingredients of good quality. Everything that nature has to offer grows in this tropical paradise, as Thailand is also known: herbs and spices in extravagant quantities with their unique aroma and scent, like basil, cilantro, lemongrass, ginger, galangal, garlic, limes and chili peppers. They are an important ingredient of those indispensable curry pastes that every good Thai housewife naturally makes herself. Here, they are available ready-made in Asian food stores. Exotic fruits and vegetables, like papayas, pineapples, eggplants, coconuts and sprouts, all contribute to the delicate balance of aromas that the Thai kitchen is famous for. With there being a vast number of rivers in Thailand – which itself is partly surrounded by the sea – it is natural that fish is top of the list as a source of protein. Meat in Thailand is usually eaten as poultry, particularly chicken. The most important ingredient, however, and this applies all over Asia, is rice. Whether as aromatic rice, sticky rice, or long-grain rice, it is the central focus of each dinner-table. Consequently, an invitation to a meal is a "khin khao", or "come and eat rice".

1

PINEAPPLE (left) is native to South America, but has been cultivated in Thailand for centuries. When ripe, the smell is very strong at the bottom. The outer skin should be golden brown and not have any green.

1 CILANTRO LEAVES are a firm favorite of Thai cooking. The fine-leafed cilantro, that somewhat resembles flat leaf parsley, is chopped and added to meals. It has a spicy flavor with anise overtones.

2 GINGER ROOT is a basic of Thai cuisine and mostly used fresh. The flavor is peppery and slightly sweet while the aroma is pungent and spicy. The pale yellow root is peeled and then either grated or chopped.

3 **PAPAYAS** grow on trees and belong to the fig family. Ripe fruits have a yellow-green to golden-green skin and are used for desserts. Unripe green fruits are prepared like vegetables or added to salads.

4 **SOY BEAN SPROUTS** are available either fresh or canned. Fresh soy beans should always be rinsed with boiling hot water to kill any germs.

5 **COCONUT MILK** is made from the flesh of the coconut that is grated, mixed with hot water and then squeezed through a cloth.

6 **THAI EGGPLANTS** are smaller than the European ones. They come in a variety of shapes and colors.

7 **BOK CHOY,** also called Chinese mustard cabbage, is a vegetable that resembles celery, but is a member of the cabbage family. It is related to Swiss chard. It has thick, white stalks and dark green leaves.

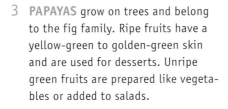

OYSTER SAUCE and FISH SAUCE are seasoning ingredients in Thai cuisine and used instead of salt (see also page 112). Shrimp paste – made from salted, dried shrimp – is used for the same purpose.

CURRY PASTES in green, red and yellow contain lots of herbs and spices and cannot be replaced by curry powder.

KAFFIR LIME LEAVES are the dark green, hourglass-shaped leaves of the kaffir lime tree, also known as makrut lime tree. They are extremely aromatic and are added to the pan whole or cut into thin strips. The bumpy fruits of the tree are not very juicy, but they have a thick, aromatic peel which, when cut into strips (zests), can also be used for seasoning.

PALM SUGAR is made from the fruits of particular palmtrees and is pale yellow to brown in color. The sugary sap is boiled until it is reduced to form a thick mixture and then dried. Palm sugar is a light golden brown paste and tastes a little like caramel.

THAI BASIL is available as three different types: Bai Horapa (sweet basil), Bai Maeng-Lak (lemon basil) and Bai Gkaprow (holy basil). The most popular one used is Bai Horapa which can be replaced by European basil.

LEMONGRASS is a reed-like plant that today is grown on plantations. The thick stalks contain essential oils with a lemon-like smell and flavor. When cooking, use only the lower, delicate part of the root, since this can be eaten when chopped very finely.

Step by Step
Thai Kitchen Basics

In Thailand food is cooked and eaten all day long. Hawkers and peddlers both on wheels or on boats sell their wares round the clock. However, the main meal of the day is eaten in the evenings with the family. For the Thai, food is part of the joy of life. The strict European distinction between appetizers, main meal and dessert is unknown here. Usually all foods are served together with a large bowl of rice. A lot of consideration is given to balancing texture, color, spices and ingredients. A mild dish balances out a spicy one, a crunchy one complements a saucy one, a grilled dish a steamed one. And everything is prepared in the Asian all-round kitchen utensil – the wok. But before that, all the ingredients are chopped up into really small pieces so that cooking times are kept short. In Thailand you eat with a spoon and fork, whereby the spoon is taken to the mouth. Knives are not needed for cutting. Chopsticks are only used for certain noodle meals.

Preparing spring rolls

1 Soak rice paper in tepid water for a few seconds until soft. Place on a clean dishtowel to rest for 2 minutes. Allow frozen sheets of spring roll pastry to defrost.

2 Put 1 tablespoon filling onto the lower third of each sheet.

3 Fold the sheet of pastry over the filling and roll into a cylindrical shape half way up.

4 Fold the left and right edges inward and continue rolling up the sheets of pastry. Brush the ends of the pastry with egg white and press together firmly.

5 Deep-fry the spring rolls for 2-3 minutes each in a little hot oil until golden yellow. Spring rolls made of rice paper are eaten fresh or steamed.

6 Remove the fried spring rolls from the oil and allow to drain on a paper towel. Keep warm in the oven until all are done.

Preparing Thai Chili Sauce

1 Rinse and peel ½ red bell pepper; dice finely. Peel 1 garlic clove and cut into small pieces. Prepare and seed 2 fresh chili peppers, wash and cut up into small pieces.

2 With a mortar and pestle, crush all the ingredients for a few minutes until the paste is smooth.

3 Put all the ingredients in a pan with 1 cup water, 5 tablespoons rice vinegar and 5 tablespoons sugar and bring to a boil, stirring constantly.

4 Cook for about 30 minutes without a lid until the sauce thickens. Fill into a small bowl. Chill before serving.

Preparing lemongrass

1 Cut the outer leaves from the lemongrass stalks and remove the dried upper half. Wash the stalks and pat dry.

2 To eat raw, chop the stalks very finely with a kitchen knife. To cook, cut the stalks into pieces and remove before serving.

Cooking scented rice

1 Rinse Thai scented rice or jasmine rice well in a sieve until all the starch has been washed out and the water runs pure. Allow to drain.

2 Fill the rice into a pan and add water (about 3 cups water for 1 ⅓ cups rice or according to package instructions). The water should cover the rice by ¾ inch.

3 Cover the rice and bring to a boil, then cook for about 25 minutes over low heat until the rice has absorbed all the water.

4 At the end of the cooking time, leave the pan to sit, still covered, for another 5 minutes. If the rice is to be fried, allow to cool well before use.

Snacks
and Salads

Chicken Satay
with Peanut Sauce

A must for all Thai fans: Although satay used to be an Indonesian speciality, the Thai version has become a classic appetizer

Ingredients

1 1/4 pounds boneless, skinless chicken breast portions

2 garlic cloves

1 piece fresh ginger root (size of a hazelnut)

1 stalk lemongrass

1/4 teaspoon ground cumin

1 1/4 teaspoon ground coriander seeds

1 1/2 cups unsweetened coconut milk · 3 teaspoons sugar

2 teaspoons curry powder

salt · 4 ounces peeled, unsalted peanuts

1 red chili pepper

1 tablespoon Asian red curry paste (store-bought)

2 tablespoons lime juice

1 tablespoon peanut butter

Preparation

SERVES 4

1 Wash the chicken, dab dry and cut into 1 1/4-inch strips. Soak about 50 wooden skewers in water for 30 minutes so that they don't burn during barbecueing.

2 Peel the garlic and ginger and dice finely. Prepare the lemongrass, wash and chop finely. Mix the garlic, ginger, lemongrass, 1/4 teaspoon each ground cumin and coriander with 2/3 cup coconut milk. Season with 1 teaspoon each sugar and curry and a little salt. Allow the meat to marinate in the coconut milk for about 1 hour.

3 Meanwhile prepare the sauce: Roast the peanuts in a pan without oil, allow to cool and crush with a mortar and pestle or chop very finely in a food processor. Prepare, seed and wash the chili pepper, then chop finely. Heat 3/4 cup coconut milk at a medium temperature and stir in the curry paste. Gradually add the peanuts, chili pepper, 1 teaspoon coriander, 1 teaspoon curry, lime juice, 2 teaspoons sugar and peanut butter. Allow the sauce to cook for about 2 minutes. It should be creamy. Remove the sauce from the heat and season to taste. Allow to cool.

4 Remove the chicken from the marinade, allow to dry slightly and thread onto the skewers shaping waves. Place under the grill and grill the skewers for 10 minutes until brown, turning occasionally. Serve with the peanut sauce.

Tip

Serve with a cucumber salad: Peel 1/2 cucumber and 3 shallots and cut into small rings. Cut 1 chili pepper into rings. Mix everything with 4 tablespoons lime juice, and 1 teaspoon each salt and sugar.

Rice Paper Rolls
with Sweet and Sour Sauce

A little snack for in between: The secret of great spring rolls is to use the freshest ingredients available

Ingredients

For the rolls:

14 sheets rice paper or frozen spring roll pastry (about 8-inch squares)

3 tablespoons dried Chinese mushrooms

1 3/4 ounces glass noodles

6 ounces pork tenderloin

1 tablespoon all-purpose flour

4 ounces bean sprouts (canned)

1 carrot · 3 sprigs basil

2 sprigs mint

3 tablespoons vegetable oil

3 tablespoons dark soy sauce

5 tablespoons chicken stock

salt · 1 teaspoon cornstarch

For the sauce:

2 tomatoes · 2 garlic cloves

2/3 cup beef stock

1 tablespoon light soy sauce

4 tablespoons sugar

2 tablespoons white wine vinegar

salt · freshly ground pepper

Preparation

SERVES 4

1 Prepare the sheets of rice paper or allow frozen spring roll pastry to defrost (see page 8) and arrange the sheets beside one another. Allow the mushrooms to soak in tepid water for at least 2 hours, then squeeze dry and cut into thin strips. Cover the glass noodles with boiling hot water, allow to swell for 10 minutes, drain and cut into 2-inch lengths with scissors. Rinse the meat, dab dry and cut into 1/2-inch strips. Toss the meat in the flour.

2 Allow the bean sprouts to drain well in a sieve. Peel the carrot and cut into thin strips like the bean sprouts. Wash the herbs, shake dry, pluck off the leaves and chop coarsely.

3 Heat 2 tablespoons oil in a pan. Add the bean sprouts and carrots and stir-fry. Add the soy sauce and braise for 3 minutes. Stir-fry the meat in another pan in the remaining oil, pour in the stock, then stir in the vegetables, herbs, mushrooms and glass noodles. Season with salt. Stir the cornstarch well with a little cold water until smooth, then pour into the meat-vegetable mix to thicken.

4 Moisten the rice paper sheets with a little water. Spread the mixture along the center of the sheets, leaving an edge free all round. Fold in the sides, then roll up the sheets lengthwise. Press the ends together firmly. Fill a steam cooker with water and place the spring rolls in the steaming basket. Cover and steam for about 8 minutes.

5 For the sauce, put the tomatoes into boiling hot water for about 30 seconds, then rinse with cold water, peel, cut in half, seed and chop coarsely. Peel the garlic cloves and chop finely. Fill the tomatoes, garlic, stock, soy sauce, sugar and vinegar into a pan and simmer for about 8 minutes. Season to taste with salt and pepper. Serve with the spring rolls.

Spring Rolls
with Chicken

Ingredients

16 sheets spring roll pastry
(8-inch x 8-inch) · 1 red chili
pepper · 3 tablespoons sugar
salt · 1 tablespoon rice vinegar
3 scallions · 1 stalk lemongrass
3 garlic cloves
1 fresh green chili pepper
2 teaspoons grated lemon rind
2 teaspoons shrimp paste
1 pound 2 ounces chicken breast
4 tablespoons soy oil
3 tablespoons Thai fish sauce
1 tablespoon sugar · freshly
ground pepper · oil, for frying

Preparation
SERVES 4

1 Allow the pastry to defrost. For the dip, seed
the red chili pepper, wash and chop finely.
Bring the sugar to a boil in about 3 tablespoons water, allow to simmer until syrupy.
Stir in 1 teaspoon salt, the vinegar and chili
pepper; allow to cool.

2 Prepare the scallions and lemongrass, wash
and chop finely. Peel and chop the garlic
clove. Seed the green chili pepper, wash and
chop. Mix all with the lemon rind and shrimp
paste.

3 Wash the chicken breasts, dab dry and cut into
very small pieces. Heat the wok, add the soy oil
and sear the spice mixture. Add the chicken and
stir-fry until brown. Season to taste with fish
sauce, sugar, salt and pepper. Allow to cool
and arrange in the center of the pastry squares.

4 Fold one corner of the pastry square over the
filling. Bring the sides over the filling to the
inside. Roll up the pastry "envelope", and
press the ends together firmly. Heat the oil
and fry the rolls (in batches) for 3-4 minutes
until golden brown. Allow to drain, then serve
with the chili dip.

Thai Vegetables
in Rice Paper Wrappers

Ingredients

16 sheets rice paper
(about 8-inch x 8-inch)
16 young carrots (with greens)
2 bunches scallions
2 red chili peppers
salt · 2 tablespoons butter

Preparation

SERVES 4

1 Arrange the sheets of rice paper on kitchen towels and moisten with water. Wash the carrots and brush, do not peel. Leave on a little of the green.

2 Prepare the scallions, wash and cut crosswise into pieces about 4 3/4 inches long. Cut these pieces into thin strips lengthwise. Prepare the chili peppers, seed, wash and cut into equally thin strips.

3 Cook the carrots for about 7 minutes in boiling salted water, rinse with cold water and allow to drain. Heat the butter and braise the chili in the butter. Add the carrots, stir and salt.

4 Lay 2 sheets of rice paper on top of each other, arrange the carrots, chili strips and scallions in the center and roll up the spring rolls. Brush the edges with a little water and press together. Serve with the chili dip on page 16 (optional).

Shrimp and Pork Skewers
with Chili Sauce

Not at all askew: This mixture of ground pork and shrimp,
wrapped around a skewer, is simple but unusually delicious

Ingredients

10 ounces shrimp (peeled)

7 ounces ground pork

2 tablespoons fish sauce

1 teaspoon palm sugar

freshly ground pepper

vegetable oil, for brushing

2/3 cup sweet-hot chili sauce

2 tablespoons rice vinegar

1 bunch Asian herbs (e.g.

cilantro, Thai basil, mint)

Preparation

SERVES 4

1 Soak 8 thick wooden skewers in water for 30 minutes. Wash the shrimp and dab dry. Chop the shrimp finely and mix with the ground pork. Season with the fish sauce, the palm sugar and a little pepper.

2 Divide the meat mixture into 8 portions. Wet your hands and form long rolls. Wrap them around the skewers and press into sausage shape. Brush with oil and barbecue for 8-10 minutes on a hot grill or under the grill. Or, alternately, fry the skewers in a little oil in a skillet until brown all round.

3 Mix the chili sauce with the vinegar. Wash the herbs, shake dry and pluck the leaves from the stems. Arrange the herbs on plates, with the skewers on top. Serve with chili sauce.

Tip

Palm sugar is available from Asian food stores either in cans or compressed as cakes. It is not as sweet as white sugar. Alternately, use brown sugar instead.

Shrimp Patties
with Thai Chili Sauce

*Griddle cakes with a difference: This time the burgers
are prepared the Thai way – without meat but with shrimp instead*

Ingredients

2 pounds large shrimp

(fresh or defrosted)

1 small red chili pepper

3 garlic cloves

2 sprigs cilantro

salt · freshly ground pepper

1 egg

2 cups vegetable oil

Preparation

SERVES 4

1 Peel the shrimp, remove heads and tails. Cut open the shrimp along the back and devein. Wash the shrimp, dab dry and chop very finely. Prepare the chili pepper, seed, wash and cut into thin strips. Peel the garlic. Wash the cilantro, shake dry and pluck the leaves from the stems.

2 Crush the garlic, chili and cilantro leaves together with the salt and pepper with a mortar and pestle. Add the shrimp mixture and work everything together well to make a paste. Add the egg and mix well.

3 With wet hands, form 2 tablespoons of mixture into a patty about 2 inches across. Continue until the shrimp mixture is used up. Heat the oil, fry the shrimp patties in the oil for about 2 minutes until golden yellow, then allow to drain on paper towels. Serve with the home-made Thai chili sauce from page 9, or with a shop-bought sauce.

Tip

Asian food stores stock chili sauces with all sorts of flavorings: from spicy to sweet-hot. The store-bought chili sauces are made mainly from red chili peppers, vinegar, garlic and spices.

Wontons
with Vegetable Filling

Ingredients

20 wonton sheets (frozen, about 3-inch x 3-inch)

1 carrot · 1 stalk celery

1 3/4 ounces Chinese cabbage

1 3/4 ounces Shiitake mushrooms

1 ounce soy bean sprouts

1 3/4 ounces bamboo shoots (canned)

1 garlic clove · 1 piece ginger root (size of a hazelnut) · 2 tablespoons sesame oil · 1 tablespoon chopped cilantro · salt · freshly ground pepper · 1/2 tablespoon curry powder

1/2 tablespoon each rice vinegar and fish sauce · 2 tablespoons soy sauce · 1 leek · oil, for frying

Preparation

SERVES 4

1 Spread the sheets of wonton pastry on a damp dishtowel and allow to defrost for about 30 minutes.

2 Peel the carrot, prepare the celery, wash the Chinese cabbage and spin dry in a salad spinner. Clean the mushrooms, pour hot water over the soy bean sprouts and allow to drain. Allow the bamboo shoots to drain. Dice the vegetables very finely and mix together. Peel the garlic and press into the vegetables. Peel the ginger and chop finely.

3 Heat the sesame oil and stir-fry the vegetables in the oil. Season with the ginger, cilantro, salt, pepper, curry, rice vinegar, fish and soy sauce, then allow the mixture to cool.

4 Prepare the leek, remove the leaves and cut lenghtwise into thin strips (about 12-inch length). Blanch the leek, rinse briefly in cold water and allow to drain. Fill a little vegetable mix onto the center of the pastry sheets. Brush the edges with water and twist together above the filling. Tie with strips of leek. Heat the oil and deep-fry the wontons in the oil in batches until crunchy. Serve with chili sauce (optional).

Rice Paper Packets
with Shrimp

Ingredients

3 1/2 cups cooked, peeled shrimp

1/2 cup soy bean sprouts

3 sprigs cilantro

3 sprigs Thai basil

2 garlic cloves

8 sheets rice paper (about
4-inch squares)

1 tablespoon sesame oil

5 red chili peppers

1 tablespoon sugar

3 tablespoons rice vinegar

1 tablespoon light soy sauce

Preparation

SERVES 4

1 Wash the shrimp, dab dry and cut into small
pieces. Pour boiling hot water over the soy
sprouts and allow to drain. Chop the soy
sprouts very finely.

2 Wash the cilantro and basil and shake dry.
Pluck the leaves from the stems and chop. Peel
the garlic and chop. Arrange the sheets of rice
paper on dishtowels and moisten with water.

3 Heat the oil, add the garlic and shrimp and
stir-fry in the hot oil. Remove and mix with the
bean sprouts and herbs. Arrange the mixture
on the sheets of rice paper, bring the corners
up and twist to make packets. Tie together
with strips of leek (see page 22).

4 For the dip, prepare the chili peppers, seed,
wash and chop finely. Dissolve the sugar with
1 tablespoon water and the rice vinegar. Stir in
the chilies and soy sauce. Serve cold.

Shrimp Satay
with Pineapple

An irresistible combination: Delicate shrimp with fruity pineapple are favorites not just of seafood fans

Ingredients

½ pineapple

16-20 jumbo shrimp

(ready-to-cook)

1 tablespoon vegetable oil

⅓ cup plain full-fat yogurt

2 teaspoons curry powder

salt · freshly ground pepper

Preparation

SERVES 4

1 Cut the pineapple half into four equal parts. Remove the hard core and peel the pineapple. Cut the segments crosswise into ½-inch slices, catching the juice. Rinse the shrimp and pat dry with paper towels.

2 Thread the shrimp onto a skewer, alternating with pieces of pineapple, making 8-10 skewers. Heat the oil in a pan or wok and fry the shrimp skewers in this all round.

3 For the dip, mix the yogurt with the curry powder and the pineapple juice. Season with salt and pepper. Serve the dip in a seperate bowl together with the shrimp skewers.

Tip

If you prefer your dips hotter, stir in a finely chopped chili pepper, too. Finely chopped cilantro leaves and lime juice give the yogurt a lemony freshness.

Rice Noodle Salad
with Shrimp and Peppers

An unusual sensory perception: This refreshing salad is
perfect for tuning your guests in to the coming delicacies

Ingredients

3 ½ ounces thin rice noodles

1 red bell pepper

1 bunch cilantro

7 ounces shrimp (cooked)

4 scallions

1 teaspoon green curry paste

1 ½ tablespoons fish sauce

2 tablespoons sesame oil

about 2 tablespoons lime juice

Preparation

SERVES 4

1 Cover the rice noodles in a bowl with boiling hot water and allow to swell for 10 minutes.

2 Prepare the bell pepper, seed, wash and quarter lengthwise, then cut into thin strips crosswise. Wash the cilantro, shake dry and pluck the leaves. Rinse the shrimp in a sieve under cold running water and allow to drain. Prepare the scallions, wash and cut into rings diagonally.

3 For the marinade, mix the curry paste with about 3 tablespoons hot noodle water until smooth. Stir in the fish sauce, sesame oil and lime juice.

4 Pour the water off the rice noodles, allow to drain and cut into bite-sized pieces with scissors. In a bowl, mix the rice noodles, shrimp, peppers, scallions and cilantro. Add the marinade, toss lightly and serve the salad in small bowls.

Tip

Rice noodles, which are actually made from thin rice flour dough, are as popular in Thai cuisine as rice. Thais have them for breakfast, too. They are available fresh or dry and in various forms.

Papaya Shrimp Salad
with Chili and Cilantro

*A feast for the senses: There's something appealing for your eyes,
mouth and nose in this combination of spicy, hot and sour ingredients*

Ingredients

2 medium green papayas

2 pounds shrimp

(ready-to-cook)

2 sprigs cilantro

2 red onions

3 tablespoons vegetable oil

3 garlic cloves

5 chili peppers

2 tablespoons fish sauce

3 tablespoons lime juice

Preparation

SERVES 4

1 Cut the papayas in half lengthwise. Remove the seeds with a teaspoon and scoop out the flesh, leaving a thin edge. Reserve the papaya halves. Cut the flesh into strips.

2 Peel the shrimp, remove heads and tails. Cut shrimp open along the back and devein. Wash the shrimp and dab dry. Wash the cilantro and shake dry, pluck the leaves off the stems and chop coarsely. Peel the onions, cut in half, then into wedges.

3 Heat the oil in a pan and stir-fry the shrimp in the oil for about 2 minutes until pink. Remove from the pan, mix with the flesh of the papaya, the onions and cilantro and fill into the hollowed-out papaya halves.

4 Peel the garlic. Prepare the chili peppers, seed and wash. Chop garlic and chili peppers finely. Mix the fish sauce, lime juice, garlic and chili together well to make a dressing and pour over the salad. Mix everything together carefully once more.

Tip

If you can only buy unripe green papayas, use these. They are crunchy fresh and taste very similar to tart apples. But the salad also tastes good with ripe papayas.

Vegetable Salad
with Peanut Coconut Sauce

Ingredients

1 red and 1 green bell pepper

1 garlic clove · 1 red onion

1 small zucchini · 1 carrot

2 cups drained, canned bamboo shoots

1 bunch cilantro

$1/3$ cup chopped peanuts

2-3 tablespoons lime juice

$2/3$-inch piece of fresh ginger root

$3/4$ cups unsalted peanuts

1 cup unsweetened coconut milk (canned)

1-2 teaspoons red curry paste

1 teaspoon palm sugar

2 tablespoons fish sauce · salt

Preparation

SERVES 4

1 Prepare the bell peppers, seed, wash and cut into fine strips. Peel the garlic and onion, chop the garlic, cut the onion into strips.

2 Prepare the zucchini, wash well, cut in half, seed and cut into strips. Peel the carrot and also cut into strips. Allow the bamboo shoots to drain in a sieve. Wash the cilantro, shake dry, pluck the leaves from the stems and chop coarsely.

3 Mix the strips of bell pepper, zucchini, onions and carrot with the garlic, bamboo shoots, cilantro and chopped peanuts. Drizzle with 1 tablespoon lime juice.

4 For the peanut-coconut sauce, peel the ginger root and chop or grate. Grind the peanuts in a mixer or chop finely. Mix the ginger and nuts with the coconut milk, curry paste, sugar and fish sauce and bring to a boil. Allow to thicken for about 15 minutes. Season to taste with the remaining lime juice and salt. Serve with the salad or sprinkle over and mix in.

Glass Noodle Salad
with Cucumber and Peppers

Ingredients

3 ½ ounces glass noodles

7 ounces cucumber

1 red bell pepper

3 ½ ounces soy bean sprouts

½-inch piece fresh ginger root

2 teaspoons vegetable oil

1 tablespoon white wine vinegar

2 teaspoons light soy sauce

2 tablespoons orange juice

2 tablespoons lemon juice

3 tablespoons chopped cilantro
leaves

Preparation

SERVES 4

1 Cover the glass noodles in a bowl with boiling hot water and allow to swell for 10 minutes. Pour into a sieve, rinse with cold water and allow to drain.

2 Wash the cucumber well, first cut crosswise into ¼-inch pieces, then cut into strips. Prepare the bell pepper, seed, wash and cut into 1 ½-inch strips. Pour the soy bean sprouts into a sieve and pour boiling water over, then rinse with cold water and allow to drain.

3 Peel the ginger and chop very finely. Mix with oil, white wine vinegar, soy sauce, orange and lemon juice for the dressing.

4 Mix the glass noodles with the soy bean sprouts, the strips of cucumber and peppers. Stir the dressing under, sprinkle the chopped cilantro leaves over the salad and serve.

Rice Noodle Salad
with Ground Meat

*An interchange of contrasts: Velvety noodles, spicy ground
meat and crunchy vegetables tickle the taste buds at every bite*

Ingredients

7 ounces wide rice noodles

3-4 leaves Chinese cabbage

1 red bell pepper

1 tomato

2 shallots

3 garlic cloves

2 tablespoons peanut oil

10 ounces ground meat

salt · freshly ground pepper

1 egg

½ bunch cilantro

¼ cup cashew nuts

2 tablespoons fish sauce

1 tablespoon lime juice

2 tablespoons vinegar

½ teaspoon Sambal Oelek

sugar · 1 lime

Preparation

SERVES 4

1 Soak the rice noodles in boiling hot water and allow to swell for 10 minutes. Pour into a sieve and allow to drain.

2 Wash the leaves of Chinese cabbage, shake dry and cut into strips. Prepare the bell pepper, seed, wash and dice finely. Wash the tomato, cut in half, seed and also dice. Peel the shallots and garlic, and chop finely.

3 Heat the oil in a hot wok or in a hot pan, add the meat and stir-fry over high heat for about 5 minutes. Add the shallots and garlic and fry all together for a few minutes. Season with salt and pepper, remove from the heat and set aside.

4 Whisk the egg, allow to set in a hot pan, stirring constantly, and put aside.

5 Wash the cilantro, shake dry, pluck the leaves from the stems and cut into strips. Chop the cashew nuts coarsely. Stir the fish sauce, lime juice, vinegar, 2 tablespoons water, Sambal Oelek and a little salt together.

6 Rinse the lime under hot water, rub dry and cut into wedges. Mix the rice noodles, Chinese cabbage, bell pepper, tomato, ground meat, egg, cashew nuts and cilantro with the salad dressing. Arrange on plates, garnished with lime wedges. Serve immediately.

Beef Salad
with Rice Noodles

*With a gentle bite: Whether made of rice or wheat flour – noodles
are at home the whole world over and are served both hot and cold*

Ingredients

12 ounces loin of beef

2 tablespoons fish sauce

3 garlic cloves

1 cup trimmed green beans

salt · 1 stalk celery

1 red chili pepper

7 ounces rice noodles

4 tablespoons vegetable oil

2-3 tablespoons light

soy sauce

cilantro leaves

lemon balm leaves

Preparation

SERVES 4

1 Cut the meat into bitesize pieces and season with the fish sauce. Allow to marinate while preparing the rest.

2 Peel the garlic and chop finely. Trim the beans, wash and cut into small pieces, blanch for about 3 minutes in boiling salted water. Rinse quickly with cold water and allow to drain. Prepare the stalk of celery, wash and cut into strips. Prepare the chili pepper, seed, wash and cut into small pieces.

3 Cover the rice noodles in a bowl with boiling hot water and allow to swell for 10 minutes. Rinse with cold water and allow to drain. Heat the oil in a large pan. Stir-fry the meat in the oil, then add the vegetables, garlic and chili pepper. Fry for about 3 minutes over medium heat. Allow to cool.

4 Add the rice noodles and the soy sauce to the meat and vegetables and toss lightly. Serve garnished with cilantro and lemon balm leaves.

Tip

This salad can also be served as a warm main meal. In this case increase the quantity by about one third, and add the noodles with the soy sauce to the meat in the pan and heat.

Duck Breast Salad
with Scallions

Ingredients

2 duck breast fillets with skin

4 garlic cloves

about 1-inch piece galangal

3 sprigs cilantro

2 shallots

3-4 kaffir lime leaves

2 scallions

3 tablespoons rice

2 lemons

2-3 tablespoons fish sauce

chili powder

mint leaves

Preparation

SERVES 4

1 Grill the duck breast fillets on both sides for 10-12 minutes under the grill of the oven. Allow to cool, then cut the meat into very small pieces.

2 Peel the garlic and galangal (a relative of ginger with a taste of lemon) and chop both very finely. Wash the cilantro, shake dry and pluck the leaves. Peel the shallots. Chop the cilantro, lime leaves and shallots very finely. Prepare the scallions, wash and cut into rings.

3 Dry-roast the rice in a pan until brown, then grind with a mortar and pestle. Mix everything together and toss lightly. Cut the lemons in half and squeeze out the juice. Season the duck mixture with lemon juice, fish sauce and chili powder just before serving. Garnish with mint leaves.

Rice Noodle Salad
with Duck and Shrimp

Ingredients

4 ½ ounces rice noodles

2 scallions

1 duck breast fillet with skin

(about ½ pound)

8 medium shrimp (peeled)

1 tablespoon vegetable oil

1 tablespoon soy oil

2 tablespoons chopped cilantro

1 tablespoon chopped mint

2 tablespoons lime juice

1 tablespoons orange juice

lime wedges, for garnishing

Preparation

SERVES 4

1 Cover the rice noodles in a bowl with boiling hot water and allow to swell for about 10 minutes. Rinse with cold water, allow to drain and cool a little. Prepare the scallions, wash and cut into small pieces.

2 Fry the duck breast fillet, skin down, until crisp, turn and fry for another 5 minutes. Remove, allow to cool and remove the skin (save the crisp skin for garnishing another dish). Cut the breast into thin slices.

3 Rinse the shrimp, dab dry and fry for about 3 minutes in the vegetable oil. Mix the soy oil, cilantro, mint, lime juice, orange juice, duck meat and shrimp. Allow everything to marinate briefly and add to the warm noodles. Toss lightly again and garnish with lime wedges before serving. Season to taste with salt and lime juice if necessary.

Soups and Vegetables

Coconut Milk Soup
with Shrimp

Sheer joie-de-vivre: Soups see the start of the day in Thailand,
but even in the evening this coconut milk soup is an absolute delight

Ingredients

4 scallions

1 ounce fresh ginger root

2 red chili peppers

10 ounces tomatoes

5 ounces shrimp (cooked)

1 tablespoon vegetable oil

1 cup unsweetened coconut

milk

2 ²/₃ cups vegetable stock

3 tablespoons light soy sauce

2 tablespoons lime juice

Preparation

SERVES 4

1 Prepare the scallions and wash. Cut the green diagonally into thin rings for garnishing and reserve. Chop the white of the scallions finely. Peel and chop the ginger. Prepare the chili peppers, seed, wash and chop finely.

2 Cut an X into top and bottom of the tomatoes. Put into boiling hot water for a few seconds, then rinse with cold water. The skin should come off now. Peel, halve, seed and finely dice. Rinse the shrimp in a sieve with cold water and allow to drain.

3 Heat the oil in a pan. Stir-fry the scallions, ginger and chili in the pan. Add the coconut milk and stock, briefly bring to a boil and allow to simmer for 4 minutes. Add the shrimp and diced tomatoes to the soup and heat slowly.

4 Season the soup to taste with soy sauce and lime juice. Serve with the green of the scallions.

Tip

Thai cuisine prefers the light soy sauce to the dark. It is milder than the dark sauce and doesn't change the color of the foods so much.

Rice Noodle Soup
with Chicken

A perky Thai recipe: Rice noodle soup with delicious morsels
of chicken is the perfect pick-me-up after a hard working day

Ingredients

3 ½ ounces rice noodles

3 garlic cloves

3 tablespoons vegetable oil

½ iceberg lettuce

2 celery stalks (with green)

1 scallion · 3 sprigs cilantro

scant 1 cup soy bean sprouts

7 ounces skinless, boneless
chicken breast

3 cups chicken stock

3 tablespoons vinegar

1 tablespoon sugar

4 tablespoons fish sauce

1 tablespoon dark soy sauce

2 star anise

1 tablespoon pickled radish
(canned)

freshly ground pepper

Preparation

SERVES 4

1 Cover the rice noodles in a bowl with boiling hot water and leave to swell for about 10 minutes. Pour into a sieve and rinse with cold water. Allow to drain and cut into 4-inch lengths with scissors.

2 Peel the garlic cloves and dice finely. Heat the oil in a small pan, add the garlic and stir-fry until golden yellow, then remove and set aside.

3 Prepare and wash the iceberg lettuce, dry in a salad spinner and cut into bitesize pieces. Prepare the celery, wash, then cut stalks and green into small pieces separately. Prepare the scallions, wash and cut into thin rings. Wash the cilantro, shake dry, pluck off the leaves and chop finely.

4 Put the bean sprouts in a strainer, pour over boiling hot water and allow to drain. Wash the chicken breasts, pat dry and cut into thin strips.

5 Heat the chicken stock. Add the vinegar, sugar, fish sauce, soy sauce, star anise, radish and celery and bring to a boil briefly. Add the chicken to the stock and allow to simmer for 2-3 minutes.

6 Arrange the rice noodles in soup bowls with the iceberg lettuce, cilantro, scallions, celery leaves and bean sprouts, then pour the hot chicken stock over. Season with the fried garlic and freshly ground pepper.

Scallop Soup
with Lemongrass

Ingredients

1 stalk lemongrass

1/2 red chili pepper

1-inch piece of fresh ginger root

4 cups fish stock

1 1/2 tablespoons fish sauce

1 tablespoon lime juice

salt · freshly ground pepper

2 tablespoons vegetable oil

4 shucked scallops

a few Thai basil leaves

a few cilantro leaves

Preparation

SERVES 4

1 Remove the outer leaves of the lemongrass and chop the stalk finely. Prepare the chili pepper, seed, wash and cut into thin rings. Peel and finely slice the ginger.

2 Bring lemongrass, chili pepper and fish stock to the boil, add fish sauce and ginger and simmer for about 10 minutes. Season to taste with lime juice, salt and pepper.

3 Heat the oil in a pan and stir-fry the scallops in the oil for about 1 minute on either side (or grill briefly, as preferred). Remove and allow to cool. Add the scallops to the hot soup and heat for about another 10 seconds. Wash the basil and cilantro leaves and shake dry.

4 Arrange the soup in deep bowls and garnish with basil and cilantro just before serving.

Shrimp Soup
with Mushrooms and Limes

Ingredients

1 ¼ pounds fresh shrimp

1 red chili pepper

1 tablespoon vegetable oil

1 handful enoki mushrooms

(or white mushrooms)

½ lime

2 teaspoons ground turmeric

2 tablespoons fish sauce

2 tablespoons lime juice

2 teaspoons brown sugar

a few fresh cilantro leaves

Preparation
SERVES 4

1 Peel the shrimp, cut open along the back and devein, leaving the tails complete. Wash the shrimp and dab dry. Prepare the chili pepper, seed, wash and chop finely.

2 Heat the oil in a large pot, add the shells and heads of the shrimp and sear for about 10 minutes over medium heat, stirring constantly, until the shells and heads have turned orange.

3 Add 1 cup water and simmer for 5 minutes. Add another 5 cups water and simmer for 20 minutes. Prepare the mushrooms and cut small if required. Wash the lime, rub dry and slice.

4 Strain the stock, then return to the pot, add the turmeric and chili and cook for 2 minutes. Add the shrimp to the stock and cook for another 5 minutes. Stir in the fish sauce, lime juice and sugar, add the mushrooms and lime slices, sprinkle with cilantro leaves and serve immediately.

Lemongrass Soup
with Shrimp

Lemongrass and lime leaves add a fruity freshness to
the soup. They are for flavor only and should not be eaten

Ingredients

2 stalks lemongrass

1 ¼ pounds chicken bony parts

(backs, necks)

1 clove

4 coriander seeds

3 kaffir lime leaves

salt · freshly ground pepper

sugar

4 shrimp (peeled and cooked)

1 lime

Preparation

SERVES 4

1 Prepare the lemongrass, wash and slice finely. Wash the chicken parts and fill into a pot. Add 6 cups water and the clove, coriander seeds, lime leaves and lemongrass.

2 Bring to a boil and leave to simmer for about 2 hours. Pour the stock through a sieve lined with a dish towel, remove the fat if preferred, bring to a boil again and season with salt, pepper and a pinch of salt. Wash the shrimp and dab dry. Add to the soup and heat for another 3 minutes.

3 Wash the limes with hot water, rub dry and cut in half. Cut one half into thin slices. Peel the other half very finely and cut into thin strips. Squeeze out the lime half and stir the juice into the soup.

4 To serve, arrange the lime slices and peel strips in small bowls, add the hot soup and 1 shrimp each.

Tip

If time is critical, you can use instant chicken stock. You will enhance the spicy flavor of the soup by adding thinly cut rings of chili pepper.

Fish Soup
with Noodles and Ginger

Noodle soups are often considered a full meal in Thailand:
Cilantro and ginger add to intense flavor of the fish soup

Ingredients

2 red chili peppers

1 pound fillet of fish

(e.g. snapper, rosefish or cod)

5 ounces shrimp (peeled and

cooked)

1 handful spinach leaves

1-inch piece fresh ginger root

1 tablespoon vegetable oil

3 2/3 cups vegetable stock

3 1/2 ounces thin egg noodles

1 lime

3 tablespoons light soy sauce

2 tablespoons lime juice

1 tablespoon chopped cilantro

Preparation

SERVES 4

1 Prepare the chili peppers, seed, wash and chop finely. Rinse the fillet of fish, pat dry and cut into bitesize pieces. Rinse the shrimp and allow to drain. Prepare the spinach and wash. Peel the ginger and chop.

2 Heat the oil in a pot, add the ginger and chili peppers and stir-fry. Add the vegetable stock and heat. Add the noodles and cook as given on the package until tender but still firm to the bite. Wash the lime, rub dry and cut into segments.

3 Add the shrimp, the fish and the spinach to the soup and simmer for 3-4 minutes. Season the soup to taste with soy sauce and lime juice, garnish with cilantro leaves and lime wedges and serve.

Tip

Instead of ginger, vary the flavor by sometimes using galangal, a relative of ginger. The root is said to have medicinal properties and to stimulate digestion. Young galangal tastes of lemon.

Chicken Soup
with Galangal and Mushrooms

Ingredients

2 stalks lemongrass

2-inch piece galangal

3 kaffir lime leaves

9 ounces oyster mushrooms

2 medium tomatoes

3 fresh red chili peppers

1 1/4 pounds boneless chicken breast

1 2/3 cups unsweetened coconut milk

a few Thai basil leaves

4 tablespoons lime juice

4 tablespoons fish sauce

Preparation

SERVES 4

1 Prepare the lemongrass, wash and cut into 1-inch pieces. Peel the galangal and cut into thin slices. Wash the lime leaves and pat dry. Clean the mushrooms and cut into bitesize pieces.

2 Wash the tomatoes and quarter. Prepare the chili peppers, seed, wash and cut into rings. Rinse the chicken, pat dry and cut into strips 1/2 inch wide and 1 1/2 long.

3 Heat the coconut milk in a pot. Add the lemongrass, slices of galangal and lime leaves. Bring to a boil uncovered over medium heat and allow to simmer for 2 minutes. Add 3 cups water and heat.

4 Add the chicken strips, mushrooms and quartered tomatoes. Allow to simmer for about 5 minutes. Remove the galangal and the lime leaves. Wash the Thai basil and dab dry. Fill the chili rings, lime juice and fish sauce into soup bowls, pour the hot soup over, garnish with basil leaves and serve.

Chicken Soup
with Chilis and Pumpkin

Ingredients

1 medium onion

2 red chili peppers

about 11 ounces pumpkin

2 skinless, boneless chicken
breasts (about 7 ounces each)

1 tablespoon vegetable oil

1-2 tablespoons green curry paste

2 teaspoon ground turmeric

1 $2/3$ cups buttermilk

2 tablespoons fish sauce

2 tablespoons lime juice

2 tablespoons brown sugar

a few leaves Thai basil

Preparation
SERVES 4

1 Peel the onion and dice finely. Prepare the
chili peppers, seed, wash and chop finely.
Peel the pumpkin and dice. Rinse the chicken
breast, pat dry and cut into bitesize pieces.

2 Heat the oil in a large wok. Add the onion,
chili peppers, curry paste and turmeric and
stir-fry for about 3 minutes over medium heat.

3 Add the buttermilk and 1 cup water, bring to a
boil, turn the heat down and simmer uncovered
for about 5 minutes.

4 Add the pumpkin and cook for 10 minutes.
Then add the chicken and simmer for another
8 minutes, stirring occasionally.

5 Season the soup to taste with fish sauce, lime
juice and sugar. Wash the basil, shake dry and
add to the soup.

Vegetable Soup
with Noodles and Cilantro

Each spoon a crunchy delight: The vegetables provide
the bite, the roasted garlic the unique flavoring

Ingredients

2 garlic cloves

2 teaspoons vegetable oil

2 cups trimmed green beans
(fresh or frozen)

3 scallions · 3 1/2 ounces rice
or thin noodles

1 handful fresh soy bean
sprouts

3 cups meat or vegetable
stock · 1-2 tablespoons light
soy sauce · 1-2 tablespoons
lime or lemon juice

1 tablespoon sesame oil

salt · freshly ground pepper

2 tablespoons cilantro leaves

Preparation

SERVES 4

1 Peel the garlic and dice or slice finely. Heat the oil, add the garlic and fry until golden brown.

2 Trim the green beans, wash and cut diagonally, making about 1/2-inch lengths (allow frozen green beans to defrost in the fridge one day before). Prepare the scallions, wash and cut diagonally into 1/2-inch pieces.

3 Cover the noodles in a bowl with boiling hot water and allow to swell for 10 minutes. Pour into a sieve, rinse with cold water and allow to drain. Keep warm. In boiling water cook first the bean sprouts for 1 minute, then the beans for 4 minutes until done. Rinse briefly under cold running water and allow to drain. Heat the stock and bring to a boil.

4 Arrange the noodles, beans, onions and sprouts in deep plates or bowls. Season the stock with soy sauce, lime or lemon juice, sesame oil, salt and pepper. Pour over the ingredients. Sprinkle the roast garlic and cilantro leaves over the soup and serve.

Tip

Roast garlic adds spice and crunch to the soup. But be sure it is not roasted too strongly or becomes too dark, since it will then become bitter.

Seafood Soup
with Lemongrass

There is no need to fish for compliments: Everything the oceans can provide is delightfully enhanced by lemongrass

Ingredients

3 ½ ounces each jumbo shrimp, blue mussels, fillet of fish and squid

1 tomato

2 scallops

4 garlic cloves

2 dried chili peppers

2 stalks lemongrass

2-inch piece galangal

4 cups meat or vegetable stock

5 kaffir lime leaves

2 teaspoons sugar

2 sprigs dill

Preparation

SERVES 4

1 Peel the shrimp, leaving on the tails. Cut open along the back and devein. Rinse the shrimp and pat dry. Brush the mussels under cold running water, discarding the closed ones. Wash the fish and squid, pat dry and cut into bitesize pieces.

2 Wash the tomato, cut in half, seed and then cut into eight equal parts. Peel the shallots and garlic and chop finely. Sear in a pan without oil with the chili peppers. Allow to cool, then crush lightly with a mortar and pestle.

3 Braise the mussels in a pan with little water until they open. Shuck the meat, discarding all unopened mussels.

4 Reserve a small piece of lemongrass. Pound the remaining lemongrass and the galangal flat. Bring the stock to a boil. Add the fish, tomato, shallot-garlic-chili mixture, lemongrass, galangal, 3 lime leaves, sugar and half the dill. Cook everything for about 4 minutes.

5 Halve the remaining lime leaves, crush the reserved piece of lemongrass and separate into fibers. Arrange both in 4 soup bowls. Pluck the tips of the dill. Add the shrimp, mussels and squid to the soup and allow to simmer for a few minutes until done. Fill the soup into the bowls, sprinkle dill over and serve.

Wonton Soup
with Spinach and Carrots

Ingredients

16 sheets wonton pastry (frozen, about 3-inch squares)

1 1/4 cups (5 1/4 ounces) leaf spinach

salt · 1 garlic clove

2 1/2 ounces ground meat

freshly ground white pepper

1 1/2 tablespoons fish sauce

1 egg white · 1 large carrot

1 tablespoon vegetable oil

3 cups vegetable stock

1 teaspoon Sichuan peppercorns

1 teaspoon lemon juice

2 sprigs Thai basil

Preparation
SERVES 4

1 Allow the sheets of pastry to defrost. Prepare the spinach, wash and blanch briefly in hot salted water. Rinse quickly in cold water, allow to drain and chop finely. Peel the garlic clove and chop. Mix with the ground meat and fish sauce to make a filling. Season with white pepper.

2 Brush the sheets of pastry with the egg white. Place a little filling in the middle of each sheet. Fold one side diagonally over the other and press the edges together firmly.

3 Bring a generous amount of lightly salted water to a boil, add the pastry packets and allow to simmer for 5 minutes. Remove with a ladle and keep warm.

4 Peel the carrot, carving narrow grooves all round lenghtwise (with a knife or zester), then slice. Heat the oil, add the carrot slices and stir-fry. Add the stock, spinach and Szechuan peppercorns, cover and cook for 3 minutes. Add the stuffed wontons to the soup and season to taste with lemon juice. Wash the basil, shake dry, pluck the leaves and use to garnish the soup.

Hot Cucumber Soup
with Bell Peppers

Ingredients

1 1/3 cups cucumber (peeled and
sliced)

2 yellow bell peppers

2-3 tablespoons vegetable oil

3 cups vegetable stock

3 tablespoons soy sauce

juice of 1 lime

2 tablespoons sesame oil

1 teaspoon ground paprika
(extra hot)

salt · freshly ground pepper

2 tablespoons hot chili sauce
(from an Asian food store)

3 tablespoons chopped chives

Preparation

SERVES 4

1 Peel the cucumber, slice lengthways, then cut
into strips. Seed the peppers, wash and dice
finely.

2 Heat the oil in the wok, add the bell peppers
and stir-fry for about 3 minutes until done.
Add the diced cucumber.

3 Add the vegetable stock, soy sauce, lime juice,
sesame oil and ground paprika, stir in, cover
and allow to cook for 3 minutes. Season with
salt, pepper and chili sauce.

4 Arrange the soup in bowls, sprinkle with
chopped chives and serve.

Hot Thai Pickles
with Mango and Papaya

Some like it hot: These hot pickled vegetables combined with
exotic fruits are really much, much more than a side dish

Ingredients

about 4 1/2 ounces each
papaya and mango

5 1/4 ounces white radish

2 carrots

2 stalks celery

1 bunch scallions

3 red chili peppers

3 garlic cloves

1-inch piece fresh ginger root

1 cup rice vinegar

1 cup Thai fish sauce

1/2 cup brown sugar

Preparation

SERVES 4

1 Peel the papaya and mango and slice thinly. Prepare the radish and carrots, peel and also slice thinly. Prepare and wash the celery. Reserve the leaves for garnishing. Cut the celery into small pieces. Prepare the scallions, wash and cut coarsely. Layer the vegetables in a high bowl rinsed with hot water.

2 Prepare the chili peppers, seed, wash and cut into rings or strips. Also peel the garlic and ginger and chop finely. Bring the rice vinegar and fish sauce to the boil in a pan with the chili peppers, garlic, ginger and sugar and pour over the vegetables.

3 Allow the vegetables to cool, cover and leave in the fridge to marinate overnight. Garnish with celery leaves. The pickles go well with grilled or stir-fried meat.

Tip

White rice vinegar is made from fermented rice. The Thai variety is milder than the Chinese or Japanese rice vinegars. For variation, substitute with a slightly diluted fruit vinegar.

Rice Noodles
with Thai Basil

An ingenious invention: The Asian answer to Italian pasta
is rice noodles – a favorite side dish of the Thai besides rice

Ingredients

7 ounces wide rice noodles

4 garlic cloves

4 shallots

2 each red and green
chili peppers

2 sprigs Thai basil

½ pound beef tenderloin

4 tablespoons vegetable oil

salt

2 tablespoons oyster sauce

2 tablespoons fish sauce

1 tablespoon sugar

1 tablespoon vinegar

1 teaspoon beef stock
granules or ½ bouillon cube

Preparation

SERVES 4

1   Cover the rice noodles in a bowl with boiling hot water and allow to swell for 10 minutes. Pour into a sieve, rinse with cold water and allow to drain. Then cut into 4-inch lengths with scissors.

2   Peel the garlic cloves and shallots, wash the chili peppers and remove the stems. Mix to a paste in a food processor or mortar.

3   Wash the basil, pat dry, pluck the leaves from the stems and chop coarsely. Rinse the meat, pat dry and cut into thin strips.

4   Heat the oil in a hot wok and sear the garlic paste, stirring constantly, until the aroma develops fully. Add the meat, season with salt and stir-fry. Stir in the rice noodles.

5   Add the oyster sauce, fish sauce, sugar, vinegar and stock granules with a little water and heat for 1 minute, stirring constantly. Sprinkle with basil, stir under briefly, and serve the noodles immediately.

Tip

Thai basil has a more intense flavor than the originally European basil. It is also known as sweet basil. If it is not available, Western basil can be used as a substitute, although it tastes different.

Fried Rice
with Vegetables and Eggs

Ingredients

1 ⅓ cups long-grain or
basmati rice

salt

3 garlic cloves

7 ounces broccoli

1 red bell pepper

4 tablespoons vegetable oil

3 eggs

2 tablespoons fish sauce

2 tablespoons soy sauce

1 teaspoon sugar

Preparation

SERVES 4

1 Cook the rice in salt water according to the instructions on the package and allow to cool. Peel and chop the garlic. Prepare the broccoli, wash and separate into flowerets. Prepare the bell pepper, seed, wash and chop finely.

2 Heat the oil in a pan, add the garlic and stir-fry until golden yellow. Add the eggs, stir well and fry until golden brown.

3 Add the broccoli and bell pepper and continue to fry all together for about 3 minutes. Stir in the rice, heat and season to taste with fish sauce, soy sauce and sugar.

Vegetable Stir-Fry
with Pineapple and Ginger

Ingredients

2 small red chili peppers

2 carrots

6 ounces bok choy

1 pound broccoli

4 scallions

4 slices fresh pineapple

2 garlic cloves

2 tablespoons vegetable oil

1 ½ tablespoons chopped
fresh ginger root

1-2 tablespoons sugar

⅔ cup vegetable stock

3 tablespoons fish sauce

juice of 1 lime

a few sprigs Thai basil

Preparation

SERVES 4

1 Prepare the chili peppers, seed, wash and cut into rings. Peel the carrot and cut diagonally into thin slices. Prepare the bok choy, separate the leaves, wash and cut into wide strips.

2 Prepare the broccoli, wash and separate into flowerets. Peel the stalks and dice. Prepare the scallions, wash and cut diagonally into rings. Peel the pineapple slices, remove the hard core and dice the flesh coarsely.

3 Peel the garlic and chop. Heat the oil in a hot wok. Add garlic, chili and ginger, and stir-fry. Add the carrots and broccoli and fry for another 2 minutes, stirring constantly. Then add the scallions and stir-fry over medium heat for another minute.

4 Add the sugar and the stock. Stir in the bok choy, pineapple, fish sauce and lime juice, bring to a boil. Wash the Thai basil, shake dry, cut the leaves into strips and sprinkle over the vegetables. Serve in a banana leaf (optional).

Vegetable Ragout
the Thai Way

It's all in the mix: Exotic spices bring out the flavor of popular vegetables – this gives potatoes a new lease of life

Ingredients

1 ½ pounds potatoes

salt · 2 Thai egg plants

3 scallions

3 garlic cloves

4-5 tablespoons vegetable oil

4 tablespoons lime juice

2 tablespoons fish sauce

1 teaspoon sugar

2 teaspoons chili powder

4 kaffir lime leaves

Preparation

SERVES 4

1 Peel the potatoes, quarter and cook for 15-18 minutes in a generous amount of lightly salted water until tender but still firm to the bite. Allow to drain. Prepare the eggplants, wash and slice lengthwise. Prepare the scallions, wash and cut into long pieces. Peel the garlic and chop finely.

2 Heat the oil in a pan or wok and fry the slices of eggplant on both sides until golden brown. Allow to drain on paper towels. Stir-fry the garlic in the remaining oil briefly, add the potatoes and scallions, and fry all for about 2 minutes.

3 Remove the pan or wok from the heat and add the slices of eggplant. Mix the lime juice, fish sauce, sugar and chili powder together and add to the vegetables.

4 Wash the kaffir lime leaves and cut into thin strips. Add to the vegetables and toss lightly. Serve the vegetable ragout in small bowls. Season with fish sauce (optional).

Tip

Thai eggplants differ not just in size from their European counterparts, but also in color. They come either round or oval, as well as white, yellow, green and aubergine in color.

Mushroom-Vegetable Pan
with Cauliflower

Ingredients

1 ounce dried black fungus
mushrooms (also known as tree
ear mushrooms)

2 onions · 3 carrots

a few leaves bok choy

11 ounces Shiitake mushrooms

2 garlic cloves

11 ounces cauliflower flowerets

2 red chili peppers

2-3 tablespoons peanut oil

2 tablespoons sesame oil

2 teaspoons grated ginger root

3-4 tablespoons light soy sauce

$^{1}/_{2}$ cup vegetable stock

salt · freshly ground pepper

Preparation

SERVES 4

1 Wash the black fungus mushrooms thoroughly, put into a bowl, cover with boiling hot water and leave to soak for about 30 minutes.

2 Peel the onions and cut into rings. Peel or pre-pare the carrots and bok choy, wash and cut into strips. Prepare the Shiitake mushrooms and cut into strips. Peel the garlic and chop finely. Wash the cauliflower and allow to drain. Prepare the chili peppers, seed, wash and cut into rings.

3 Drain the black fungus mushrooms, wash and dab dry, then cut into small pieces. Heat the peanut oil and sesame oil in a wok or pan. Add the onions, garlic, chili peppers and ginger to the oil and stir-fry. Add the carrots, cauliflower and soaked mushrooms and fry for about 3 minutes over high heat, stirring constantly.

4 Add the Shiitake mushrooms and bok choy and fry for another 2 minutes, stirring constantly. Pour in the soy sauce and vegetable stock, bring to a boil and cook until tender but still firm to the bite. Season with salt and pepper. Serve with basmati rice.

Wok Vegetables
with Green Asparagus

Ingredients

1 red and 1 green bell pepper

1 pound small broccoli flowerets

11 ounces green asparagus

1 bunch scallions

4 tablespoons sesame oil

2 tablespoons oyster sauce

1 teaspoon soy sauce

a few sprigs cilantro

Preparation

SERVES 4

1 Prepare the bell peppers, seed, wash and cut into strips. Wash the broccoli flowerets and cut up (optional). Peel the stems and cut into small pieces.

2 Wash the asparagus, trim the ends, peel the lower third if necessary and cut the asparagus into pieces. Prepare the scallions, wash and cut the white and pale green parts into bite-size pieces.

3 Heat a little sesame oil in a wok or large pan, gradually add the vegetables – first the stalks of broccoli and the peppers, then the asparagus and broccoli flowerets, finally the scallions. Stirring constantly, fry, gradually adding more sesame oil (except for 1 tablespoon).

4 Finally season with oyster sauce and soy sauce. Wash the cilantro leaves, shake dry and sprinkle over the vegetables. Drizzle with the remaining sesame oil over.

Vegetable Rice
in Banana Leaf

*It's more than a green wrapping: The secret of cooking the rice
in the banana leaf lies in treating the ingredients gently*

Ingredients

½ cup basmati rice

3 banana leaves

1 bunch scallions

1 red bell pepper

2 ounces soy bean sprouts

1 ½-inch piece fresh ginger
root

1 garlic clove

2 tablespoons vegetable oil

3 ½ ounces mango

½ cup unsalted peanuts

4 sprigs cilantro

2 tablespoons chili sauce

2 tablespoons rice vinegar

3 tablespoons fish sauce

vegetable oil, for brushing

Preparation

SERVES 4

1 Prepare the rice according to the instructions on the package. Keep warm. Cut the banana leaves into 8 pieces and blanch for about 1 minute in boiling water. Remove, then rinse briefly under cold water.

2 Prepare the scallions, wash and cut into rings. Prepare the bell peppers, seed, wash and cut into strips. Put the soy beans into a sieve, wash and allow to drain. Peel the ginger and garlic and chop finely.

3 Heat the oil in a hot wok. Stir-fry the ginger and garlic briefly. Add the scallions, pepper and bean sprouts and fry for another 2-3 minutes, stirring constantly.

4 Dice the mango flesh, chop the peanuts coarsely. Wash the cilantro, shake dry, pluck the leaves and chop coarsely.

5 Mix the rice with the vegetables, the mango, peanuts and cilantro. Season with chili sauce, rice vinegar and fish sauce.

6 For each serving, overlap 2 banana leaf pieces, fill the rice mixture onto the leaves, fold together, and fasten the parcels with small skewers. Brush the banana packages with oil and grill for about 6 minutes on each side.

Fish and Seafood

Fish Fondue
with Rice and Chili Sauce

Home-made is best: One-pot cooking is a tradition in Asia –
the light variation is with white fish as protein supplier

Ingredients

1 ⅓ cups jasmine rice

1 ⅓ pounds mixed fillet of

fish (e.g. salmon, snapper

or cod) · 1 lime · salt

freshly ground pepper

2 bunches scallions

8 ounces baby corncobs

(pickled) · 4 ½ cups bamboo

shoots (canned) · 3 red chili

peppers · 1 ¼-inch piece fresh

ginger root · 2 garlic cloves

1 stalk lemongrass

3 sprigs cilantro

3 ¼ cups fish stock

5 tablespoons fish sauce

chili sauce

Preparation

SERVES 4

1 Prepare the rice according to the instructions on the package. Keep warm. Rinse the fish, pat dry and dice.

2 Wash the lime, rub dry, cut in half, squeeze out one half, slice the other half. Marinate the fish with 2 tablespoons lime juice, salt and pepper. Prepare the scallions, wash, cut in half lengthwise and then into 2-inch strips.

3 Allow the corncobs to drain and cut in half. Allow the bamboo sprouts to drain and cut into thin slices. Prepare the chili peppers, seed and wash. Peel the ginger and garlic and slice. Wash the lemongrass, dab dry and chop finely. Wash the cilantro and shake dry.

4 In a fondue pot, bring the fish stock to boil with ¾ cup water. Add the chili peppers, garlic, ginger, lemongrass, lime slices, cilantro and fish sauce. Cook the fillets of fish with the vegetables in wire baskets in the hot broth at the table. Serve with the chili sauce and scented rice.

Tip

For the fish fondue, choose white fish with firm flesh that doesn't fall apart so easily during cooking. The fish stock is available ready-made, so you don't need to make it yourself.

Red Bream
with Chili and Lemongrass

Thais love their fish fried whole — the sea bream here is accompanied by the wonderfully combined flavors of chili and lemongrass

Ingredients

1-2 red bream (about
2 pounds, ready-to-cook)

1 garlic clove

1 lime

4 tablespoons coconut milk

salt · freshly ground pepper

4 sprigs cilantro

3 red chili peppers

3 scallions

3 stalks lemongrass

Preparation

SERVES 4

1 Rinse the fish and pat dry. Score the fish several times on both sides diagonally, ensuring that the cuts are not too deep. Peel the garlic clove and press through a garlic press. Wash the lime with hot water, cut in half and squeeze out.

2 Mix the coconut milk with 2 tablespoons lime juice and garlic, season with salt and pepper. Brush the fish both inside and out with this marinade and allow to stand for about 10 minutes. Preheat the oven to 400°F.

3 Wash the cilantro, shake dry and chop the leaves of 3 sprigs finely. Place the remaining sprig in the fish. Prepare the chili pepper, wash and cut into thin rings. Prepare the scallions, wash and cut diagonally into rings. Remove the hard outer leaves from the lemongrass stalk and slice the lemongrass diagonally.

4 Put the fish on greaseproof paper or baking parchment. Arrange chili rings, scallions and lemongrass around the fish. Sprinkle with the remaining lime juice and the chopped cilantro. Add the squeezed-out limes to the fish, too, and close the "packages" firmly. Cook the fish for about 15 minutes in the preheated oven.

Tip

Red bream, like other sea bream varieties, has pleasant, fine flesh and can grow to 20 inches in length. This recipe could also be used for any other whole fish, such as trout or cod.

Rosefish Curry
with Pineapple and Tomatoes

Ingredients

1 cup basmati rice · salt

5 ounces cherry tomatoes

1 bunch Thai basil

8 ½ ounces pineapple (canned)

1 pound fillet of rosefish

(also known as ocean perch)

2 tablespoons lemon juice

freshly ground pepper

1 tablespoon vegetable oil

1 tablespoon red curry paste

1 ²/₃ cups unsweetened coconut milk

½ cup plain full-fat yogurt

1 teaspoon cornstarch

1 teaspoon grated lemon rind

1-2 tablespoons light soy sauce

Preparation

SERVES 4

1 Cook the rice according to the instructions on the package. Reserve.

2 Wash the tomatoes and cut in half. Wash the basil, shake dry and pluck the leaves. Allow the pineapple to drain, reserve the juice, and cut the pineapple slices into small pieces or use canned chunks. Wash the fish, pat dry and cut into bitesize pieces. Sprinkle the fish with lemon juice and season with salt and pepper.

3 Heat the oil in a hot wok and stir in the curry paste. Sear briefly, add the coconut milk, bring to a boil and allow to simmer for 2-3 minutes. Mix the yogurt with the cornstarch, then add to the soy sauce with the pineapple, pineapple juice and lemon rind. Bring to a boil and season with soy sauce.

4 Add the fish and tomatoes, bring to a boil again and allow to simmer for 2-3 minutes. Finally stir in the basil. Arrange the fish curry with the rice on a serving dish.

Wok-Fried Cod
with Noodles and Vegetables

Ingredients

8 ½ ounces thin egg noodles

1 pound fillet of cod

1 teaspoon yellow curry paste

2 tablespoons all-purpose flour

4-5 tablespoons vegetable oil

1 red chili pepper

1 ½ cups sugar-snap peas

1 cup sliced carrots

1 cup cherry tomatoes

grated rind of 1 lime

2 tablespoons chopped cilantro

2 tablespoons grated coconut

2 tablespoons peeled peanuts

Preparation

SERVES 4

1 Prepare the egg noodles according to the instructions on the package. Reserve. Rinse the cod, pat dry and cut into bitesize pieces, brush with curry paste and toss in flour. Heat the oil in the wok and fry the fish in the oil until crisp. Allow to drain and keep warm.

2 Prepare the chili pepper, seed, wash and cut into thin rings. Prepare and wash the sugar-snap peas, chop if required. Peel carrots and slice. Wash the cherry tomatoes and cut in half.

3 Add the chili pepper, carrots and sugar-snap peas to the oil in the wok and stir-fry for 2 minutes. Pour the noodles into a sieve, allow to drain and add to the wok. Continue frying for another 2-3 minutes.

4 Add the fish, cherry tomatoes, grated rind of the lime and cilantro, mix well with the noodles and cook for another 2-3 minutes. Garnish with grated coconut and peanuts. Serve hot.

Wontons
with Cod Filling

Little deep-fried fish balls with crisp wonton

pastry strips may look spiky but are nice to bite

Ingredients

10 sheets wonton pastry

(frozen, about 3-inch squares)

7 ounces fillet of cod

$\frac{1}{4}$ ounce light cream

salt · freshly ground pepper

2 $\frac{1}{2}$ cups vegetable oil, for

deep-frying

5 tablespoons olive oil

5 tablespoons white wine

vinegar

5 tablespoons vegetable stock

1-2 tablespoons honey

4 garlic cloves

1-2 red chili peppers

$\frac{1}{4}$ teaspoon chili powder

Preparation

SERVES 4

1 Arrange the wonton sheets beside one another and allow to defrost. Rinse the cod fillet, pat dry, chop or cut into very small pieces, removing any bones. Mix with the cream, season with salt and pepper. With wet hands, shape the fish mixture into small balls.

2 Cut the wonton sheets into thin strips. Put into a flat dish and toss the fish balls in this until they are completely but loosely covered with strips of pastry. Do not press the pastry into the balls.

3 Heat the oil in a hot wok and deep-fry the fish balls for 2-3 minutes until golden brown all round.

4 For the sauce, mix the olive oil with the white wine vinegar, vegetable stock and honey. Peel the garlic and chop finely. Prepare the chili pepper, seed, wash and chop finely. Add both to the sauce, stir in the chili powder and season to taste. Serve the wontons with the chili sauce.

Tip

Note the golden rule for chili peppers: the smaller, the hotter. The red birds' eye chili is an important ingredient in Thai cuisine. These red chili peppers are very hot. The green chili peppers are milder.

Crisp of Pikeperch
with Black Sesame Seeds

It's all in the packaging: This delicate fish, gently cooked in a pastry wrapping, is a very special treat

Ingredients

3 tomatoes

1 red and 1 green bell pepper

3 scallions · 1 garlic clove

4 round sheets spring roll
pastry (frozen, about 11
inches across)

2 tablespoons sesame oil

1 tablespoon tomato paste

2 tablespoons black sesame
seeds

3 tablespoons soy sauce

3 tablespoons rice vinegar

2 tablespoons breadcrumbs

1 1/2 pounds pikeperch fillet
(skinless)

salt · freshly ground pepper

1 egg yolk

6 tablespoons vegetable oil

Preparation

SERVES 4

1 Cut an X into the top of the tomatoes. Put into boiling hot water for a few seconds. The skin should come off now. Peel, cut in half and seed. Prepare the peppers, seed and wash. Prepare and wash the scallions. Dice the vegetables finely. Peel and finely chop the garlic. Arrange the sheets of spring roll pastry alongside one another and allow to defrost.

2 Heat the sesame oil and stir-fry the vegetables in the hot oil. Stir in the tomato paste, 1 tablespoon sesame seeds, soy sauce, vinegar and breadcrumbs and cook for about 5 minutes to thicken. Remove from the heat and allow to cool.

3 Wash the fish fillet, pat dry and cut into 4 equal pieces. Season with salt and pepper. Brush each pastry sheet with a quarter of the vegetable mixture, leaving a 1/2-inch edge all round. Arrange the fish pieces in the center.

4 Beat the egg yolk and brush the edges of the pastry. Fold the pastry over the fish and shape into packets, pressing the edges together firmly.

5 Heat the oil in a pan and fry the fish packets in the hot oil for about 3 minutes on each side until golden brown. Sprinkle with the remaining sesame seeds and serve immediately.

Tip

If you can't get this particular fish, use cod or perch. For variation, mix some finely chopped fresh ginger root and cilantro leaves into the fish mixture.

Ocean Perch
with Vegetables and Rice

Ingredients

1 1/4 cups whole-grain rice

salt

1 pound ocean perch fillet

2 garlic cloves

2 small zucchini

1/2 pound leek (the white and
pale green only)

2 red bell peppers

3 1/2 ounces white mushrooms

2 tablespoons vegetable oil

1 tablespoon horseradish

2-3 tablespoons soy sauce

juice and zest of 1 lime

freshly ground pepper

Preparation

SERVES 4

1 Prepare the rice according to the instructions
   on the package. Reserve.

2 Rinse the fillet of fish, dab dry and cut into
   bitesize pieces. Peel and chop the garlic finely.
   Prepare and wash the zucchini, cut into thin
   long strips. Prepare the leek, wash and cut
   into rings.

3 Prepare the bell peppers, seed, wash and cut
   into strips. Rub the mushrooms clean, not
   wetting them, then chop finely.

4 Heat the oil and fry the garlic and horseradish.
   Add the fish, sear for 2-3 minutes all round.
   Remove and keep in a warm place.

5 Stir-fry the vegetables in the oil for about
   7 minutes. Add the rice and fish, and cook for
   another 5 minutes. Season with soy sauce,
   lime juice and pepper, sprinkle with lime zest
   and serve.

Spicy Fillet of Salmon
with Bok Choy

Ingredients

4 fillets of salmon (about

7 ounces each, with skin)

2 dried chili peppers

2 tablespoons soy sauce

2 tablespoons honey

2 tablespoons balsamic vinegar

2 teaspoons sesame oil

1 1/4 pounds bok choy · salt

juice of 1 lemon

2 tablespoons clarified butter

Preparation
SERVES 4

1 Rinse the salmon, pat dry and remove any bones. Crush the chili peppers with a mortar and pestle and mix with the soy sauce, honey, balsamic vinegar and sesame oil.

2 Pour this marinade over the salmon and allow to stand for about 3 hours, turning the fish occasionally.

3 Prepare the bok choy, separate the leaves, wash, shake dry and chop (optional). Blanch for about 5 minutes in boiling salted water, remove from the water, allow to drain, season with salt and lemon juice.

4 Heat the clarified butter and gently fry the salmon fillets with the skin facing down for about 6 minutes over low heat. Do not turn. Serve the salmon with the bok choy.

Fried White Pomfret
with Thai Shallots

Pomfret is very popular in Thai cuisine and best cooked
over low to medium heat for the crispiest results

Ingredients

2 pounds pomfret

(ready-to-cook)

6 garlic cloves

4 Thai shallots

6 red and green chili peppers

salt · 4 sprigs basil

1 red and 1 green bell pepper

5-6 tablespoons vegetable oil

2 tablespoons oyster sauce

2 tablespoons light soy sauce

1 tablespoon palm sugar

Preparation

SERVES 4

1 Rinse the fish and pat dry. Peel the garlic and shallots. Prepare and rinse the chili peppers. Crush the garlic, shallots and chili peppers with 1 pinch of salt with a mortar and pestle or in a food processor.

2 Wash the basil, shake dry, pluck the leaves off the stems and chop coarsely. Prepare the bell peppers, seed, rinse and cut into bitesize pieces.

3 Heat the oil in a hot wok. Salt the fish and fry for 3-6 minutes on either side, depending on the size, over low to medium heat until crispy. Remove and keep warm.

4 Sear the crushed ingredients with a little remaining oil in the wok. Add the bell peppers, oyster sauce, soy sauce and sugar. Gradually add a little water, stirring constantly, and bring to the boil once. Season with basil. Place the fish on a hot serving plate, pour the sauce over the fish and serve immediately.

Tip

Pomfret is a member of the perch family, also known as perciformes. This fish is among the most exquisite and expensive of fish to eat. You can use monkfish or halibut as a substitute.

Seafood Ragout
with Egg Noodles

This really tastes of the sea: The ragout offers perfect conditions
for seafood – swimming in coconut milk with a light touch of curry

Ingredients

¹/₂ pound shrimp (peeled and
cooked)

¹/₂ pound squid (ready-to-cook)

¹/₂ pound fillet of fish (e.g.
ocean perch)

salt · freshly ground pepper

3-4 tablespoons lemon juice

2 onions · 2-3 garlic cloves

1 red chili pepper

2 stalks lemongrass

5 kaffir lime leaves

3-4 tablespoons sesame oil

2 cups unsweetened coconut
milk

1-2 tablespoons green curry
paste · palm sugar

3 tablespoons fish sauce

5 ounces Chinese egg noodles

sugar-snap peas and fresh mint
leaves, for garnishing

Preparation

SERVES 4

1 Rinse the shrimp, squid and fillet of fish and pat dry. Cut the squid and fish into bitesize pieces. Season the shrimp, squid and fish with salt and pepper and sprinkle with lemon juice.

2 Peel the onions and garlic cloves and chop finely. Prepare the chili peppers, seed, rinse and also chop finely. Prepare the lemongrass, wash and discard the hard upper section, slice the rest diagonally. Wash the lime leaves and dab dry.

3 Heat half the oil in the hot wok and briefly sear the onions, garlic, chili and lemongrass. Add the coconut milk and lime leaves and stir in the curry paste. Bring the sauce to a boil and simmer for 3 minutes. Remove the lime leaves. Season the sauce to taste with a little palm sugar and fish sauce.

4 Cook the egg noodles according to the instructions on the package, pour into a sieve and allow to drain. Add the fish and shrimp to the sauce and allow to simmer for 3-4 minutes.

5 Fry the squid for about 1 minute in a pan with the remaining oil. Blanch the sugar-snap peas, pouring over boiling hot water, then plunge them into cold water briefly and drain well.

6 Arrange the ragout on plates with the noodles and squid. Garnish with the sugar-snap peas and mint leaves before serving.

Fish Patties
with Herbs

Ingredients

4 sprigs cilantro

2 scallions

1 pound fillet of firm white fish
(e.g. ocean perch, cod)

2 red chili peppers

3 tablespoons cornstarch

1 tablespoon fish sauce

1 egg

1 tablespoon red curry paste

1/2 cup vegetable oil

7 ounces egg noodles

Preparation

SERVES 4

1 Wash the cilantro, shake dry, pluck off the
leaves and chop. Prepare the scallions, wash
and cut into fine rings. Rinse the fillet of fish,
pat dry and chop finely. Prepare the chili peppers, seed, wash and also chop finely.

2 Add the cornstarch, fish sauce, egg, cilantro,
curry paste, chili and scallions to the fish and
mix everything together well. With moist
hands take 2 tablespoons of the mixture at a
time and shape into small patties.

3 Heat the oil in a wok and fry the patties on
both sides until golden brown. Cook the egg
noodles in a generous amount of boiling salted
water according to the instructions on the
package. Pour into a sieve and allow to drain.

4 Serve the noodles in bowls, arrange the fish
patties on top and garnish with chili peppers
(optional). Serve with home-made Thai sauce
(see page 9).

Fish Cakes
with Ricotta Dip

Ingredients

1 ¼ pounds fillet of cod

4 scallions

1 ¼-inch piece fresh ginger root

1 tablespoon vegetable oil

⅔ cup unsweetened coconut milk

4 white bread slices · 2 egg yolks

1 tablespoon chopped dill

salt · freshly ground pepper

2 cups vegetable oil, for frying

½ red bell pepper · ½ cucumber

1 cup ricotta

2 tablespoons light cream

1 tablespoon lemon juice

1 tablespoon fish sauce

¼ teaspoon chili powder

Preparation

SERVES 4

1 Rinse the fish, pat dry and chop up small. Prepare the scallions, wash and cut into fine rings. Peel and chop the ginger.

2 Heat the oil in a pan and briefly stir-fry the scallions and ginger. Soak the bread slices in hot coconut milk. Squeeze out the bread and mix with the fish. Stir in the scallions, ginger, egg yolk and dill. Season the fish mixture with salt and pepper.

3 With moist hands, shape the mixture into 8 cakes. Heat the oil in a pot and fry the cakes for about 5 minutes all round until golden yellow.

4 For the dip, prepare the bell pepper, seed and dice. Peel the cucumber, cut in half and remove the seeds. Dice the cucumber finely. Mix the ricotta with the cream, lemon juice and fish sauce until smooth. Stir in the diced vegetables and season with pepper and chili powder. Garnish the dip with lemon zests (optional) and serve with the fish cakes.

Garlic Shrimp
with Pineapple

*For special occasions: Deep-fried shrimp with an aromatic
sauce are decoratively presented in hollowed-out pineapples*

Ingredients

1 egg white

4 tablespoons cornstarch

1 teaspoon grated fresh ginger

root · 1 teaspoon soy sauce

1 teaspoon curry powder

4-5 garlic cloves · salt

1 1/4 pound cooked, peeled

shrimp · 2 small pineapples

3 tablespoons white wine

vinegar · 1 1/2 teaspoons sugar

2 tablespoons ketjap manis

(thick sweet soy sauce)

cayenne pepper

5 tablespoons vegetable stock

3 1/2 cups vegetable oil,

for frying · 1 tablespoon

chopped fresh cilantro

Preparation

SERVES 4

1 Beat the egg white until foamy. Gradually beat in half the cornstarch, ginger, soy sauce and curry powder. Peel the garlic, chop coarsely and add to the egg white with a little salt. Rinse the shrimp, pat dry, add to the garlic mixture, cover and marinate for about 30 minutes.

2 Cut the pineapple in half lengthwise and hollow out, leaving a thick edge. Cut the flesh into small pieces, catching any juice.

3 In a pan, mix 5 tablespoons pineapple juice with vinegar, sugar, ketjap manis, cayenne pepper, stock and the remaining starch to make a sauce. Bring to a boil.

4 Heat the oil in a pan or deep fryer to 300°F. Deep-fry the shrimp for 1-2 minutes, remove from the oil and allow to drain on paper towels.

5 In a wok, heat 2 tablespoons frying oil. Sear the shrimp briefly once more, then stir in the pineapple pieces and the sauce. To serve, fill the shrimp into the hollowed-out pineapples and sprinkle with chopped cilantro leaves before serving.

Tip

If you need to prepare this quickly, you can use 7 ounces canned pineapple instead of fresh. In this case, serve the garlic shrimp in small bowls.

Shrimp Curry
with Lemongrass

An all-time favorite: These exquisite shellfish are in a class
of their own when accompanied by coconut milk and lemongrass

Ingredients

2 stalks lemongrass

1 red onion

2 green chili peppers

1 garlic clove

1/2 pound cherry tomatoes

1 bunch cilantro

9 ounces shrimp (peeled
and cooked)

1 tablespoon sesame oil

salt

1 2/3 cups unsweetened
coconut milk

Preparation

SERVES 4

1 Prepare the lemongrass and discard the hard upper part.
Wash the lemongrass stalks and cut the pale section into
thin rings. Peel the onion and dice finely. Prepare the chili
peppers, seed, rinse and chop finely. Peel the garlic and
chop very finely.

2 Rinse the cherry tomatoes and quarter. Wash the cilantro
sprigs, shake dry and pluck off the leaves. Rinse the shrimp
and pat dry.

3 Heat the oil in a hot wok and sear the lemongrass, onion,
chili peppers and garlic for a few minutes. Add the shrimp
and fry over high heat for 1-2 minutes, stirring constantly,
then salt and remove. Add the coconut milk and tomatoes to
the wok and cook for 2-3 minutes until the sauce thickens.

4 Add the shrimp and cilantro leaves and heat the sauce,
but do not allow to boil. Serve the curry with scented or
basmati rice.

Tip

Lemongrass is a reed. It gets its name from the
strong lemon scent that emanate from the stalk
when rubbed or shredded. In cooking, only the
pale, lower section is used.

Squid Rings
with Thai Basil

Ingredients

1 ¼ pounds squid (ready-to-cook)

4 red chili peppers

4 garlic cloves

4 green chili peppers

4 sprigs Thai basil

5 tablespoons vegetable oil

3 tablespoons oyster sauce

2 tablespoons fish sauce

1 tablespoon brown sugar

Preparation

SERVES 4

1 Rinse the squid, pat dry and cut into bitesize pieces. Prepare the red chili pepper, seed, rinse and dice finely. Peel the garlic and chop finely. Crush the chili pepper and garlic very finely with a mortar and pestle.

2 Prepare the green chili, rinse and chop. Wash the Thai basil, shake dry, pluck the leaves from the stems, and chop if too large.

3 Heat the oil in a hot wok and sear the red chili-garlic paste briefly. Drop in the squid and green chili peppers and fry for about 2 minutes over high heat, stirring constantly.

4 Season with oyster sauce, fish sauce and sugar. Garnish with Thai basil leaves, and serve immediately.

Wok Vegetables
with Squid

Ingredients

1 pound squid (ready-to-cook)

7 ounces sugar-snap peas

7 ounces broccoli flowerets

5 ounces mushrooms

7 ounces canned baby corncobs

3 garlic cloves

$^1/_2$ pound Chinese egg noodles

2 tablespoons sesame oil

2 teaspoons chopped fresh ginger root

4 tablespoons soy sauce

2 tablespoons oyster sauce

4 tablespoons rice wine

$^1/_2$ cup chicken stock

1 tablespoon cornstarch

Preparation

SERVES 4

1   Rinse the squid, pat dry and cut into thin strips lengthwise. Blanch briefly in boiling water, pour into a sieve and allow to drain.

2   Prepare and wash the sugar-snap peas. Wash the broccoli and divide the larger flowerets if necessary. Prepare the mushrooms, rub clean and slice. Allow the corncobs to drain in a sieve. Peel and chop the garlic cloves. Cook the egg noodles according to the instructions on the package, and allow to drain. Reserve.

3   Heat the sesame oil in a wok or large pan, and sear the garlic and ginger. Add the sugar-snap peas, broccoli and mushrooms, and fry all together for about 1-2 minutes more. Add the soy sauce, oyster sauce, rice wine and chicken stock, and allow to simmer for 1 minute.

4   Stir the cornstarch with a little cold water until smooth, add to the wok and bring to a boil again, stirring constantly. Add the squid and corncobs, mix all well, bring to a boil once more, then season to taste and serve with the egg noodles.

Fried Shrimp Skewers
with Chili Dip

*Don't they look like strange meatballs? It doesn't matter what
these skewers look like, it's the delicious shrimp flavor that counts*

Ingredients

For the dip:

¹/₂ red bell pepper

1 garlic clove

2 red chili peppers

4-5 tablespoons red
wine vinegar · 2 tablespoons
lime juice · 1 tablespoon sugar

For the skewers:

1 ¹/₄ pounds shrimp (peeled
and cooked) · 1 egg yolk

1 tablespoon cornstarch

2 tablespoons fish sauce

1 teaspoon sugar

freshly ground pepper

1 teaspoon black sesame seeds

8 stalks lemongrass (or
wooden skewers) · 1 ¹/₄ cups
vegetable oil, for frying

Preparation

SERVES 4

1 For the dip, prepare the bell pepper, seed, rinse and dice
finely. Peel the garlic and chop finely. Prepare the chili
peppers, rinse (seed if preferred, then the dip won't be so
hot) and also chop finely.

2 Put the bell pepper, garlic and chili peppers into a small pan
with scant 1 cup water. Add vinegar, lime juice and sugar,
bring to a boil and allow to simmer for about 15 minutes,
uncovered.

3 For the skewers, wash the shrimp, pat dry and dice very
finely. Mix with the egg yolk, cornstarch, fish sauce, sugar,
pepper and sesame seeds. Divide the shrimp mixture into
8 portions. Wash the lemongrass stalks and pat dry. With
wet hands, shape shrimp "sausages" and wrap them around
the lemongrass stalks, pressing firmly. If using wooden skewers, allow these to soak for 30 minutes in water beforehand.

4 Heat the oil in a hot wok. Fry the shrimp skewers in the oil
over medium heat until golden yellow, and allow to drain on
paper towels. Serve with the chili dip.

Tip

A fresh salad made from lettuce or Chinese cabbage
leaves, bok choy, soy bean sprouts and roasted
peanuts with a dressing of sesame oil and lime juice
goes well with this dish.

Poultry
and Meat

Chicken Curry
with Sugar-snap Peas

Whether red, yellow or green: Curry pastes ensure that
Thai cuisine stays hot – there's no curry without them

Ingredients

1 pound skinless, boneless
chicken breast

4 shallots

2 garlic cloves

$1/2$ pound sugar-snap peas

1 tablespoon vegetable oil

$3/4$ cup unsweetened coconut
milk

2 tablespoons red curry paste

2 tablespoons fish sauce

2 tablespoons palm sugar

2 red chili peppers

1 bunch garlic chives

Preparation

SERVES 4

1 Rinse the chicken, pat dry and dice finely. Peel the shallots and garlic and chop finely. Trim the sugar-snap peas, wash and cut in half.

2 Heat the oil in a hot wok, sear the shallots and garlic for 1 minute, stirring constantly. Add the coconut milk, stir in the curry paste and simmer for about 2 minutes.

3 Add the chicken, the fish sauce and the palm sugar, simmer all together for 3 minutes. Drop in the sugar-snap peas and continue to simmer for another 5 minutes, stirring costantly.

4 Prepare the chili peppers, seed and rinse. Chop 1 chili pepper finely, cut the other into thin rings. Wash the garlic chives, shake dry and cut into rings. Sprinkle chili peppers and garlic chives over the chicken curry before serving.

Tip

Garlic chives resemble long scallions rather than leeks or chives. The leaves taste peppery and mildly of garlic. Use scallions or spring onions as an alternative.

Lemongrass Chicken
on Rice Noodles

Mealtimes in Thailand always provide a variety of chili
sauces to choose from, from sweet and sour to spicy hot

Ingredients

For the chili sauce:

2 garlic cloves

4 tablespoons fish sauce

2 tablespoons lime juice

1 tablespoon palm sugar
(or alternately brown sugar)

1 tablespoon chili powder

For the meat:

1 pound boneless chicken breast

2 stalks lemongrass

1 red chili pepper

1 onion · 1 garlic clove

1 tablespoon vegetable oil

1 tablespoon yellow curry paste

$2/3$ cup unsweetened coconut
milk

3 $1/2$ ounces salted peanuts

4 tablespoons fish sauce

2 tablespoons lime juice

1 tablespoon palm sugar

$1/2$ cucumber

11 ounces thin rice noodles

Preparation

SERVES 4

1 For the chili sauce, peel the garlic and crush with a mortar and pestle. Add the fish sauce, lime juice, sugar, and chili powder and mix everything together well.

2 Rinse the chicken breast, pat dry and cut into bitesize pieces. Trim the lemongrass, wash and cut the lower pale section into thin rings. Prepare the chili peppers, seed, rinse and dice finely. Peel the onion and garlic, and also dice finely.

3 Heat the oil in a hot wok and sear the onion and garlic. Add the curry paste and 2 tablespoons coconut milk, and heat, stirring constantly.

4 Add the chicken and lemongrass and fry for about 5 minutes. Top up with the remaining coconut milk, chili pepper and peanuts. Allow to simmer over low heat for another 3 minutes. Season to taste with fish sauce, lime juice and sugar.

5 Wash the cucumber, cut in half and remove the seeds with a spoon, then slice the cucumber. Cook the rice noodles according to the instructions on the package, pour into a sieve and allow to drain.

6 Arrange the noodles in bowls. Pour the cucumber slices and chicken over the noodles. Serve the chili sauce separately.

Red Chicken Curry
with Cherry Tomatoes

Ingredients

1 1/4 pounds skinless, boneless chicken breast

7 ounces cherry tomatoes

7 ounces pineapple flesh

2 stalks lemongrass

1 tablespoon vegetable oil

1-2 tablespoons red curry paste

1 2/3 cups unsweetened coconut milk

1 tablespoon brown sugar

3 tablespoons fish sauce

2 tablespoons lime juice

Preparation

SERVES 4

1 Rinse the chicken, pat dry and cut into 1/2-inch pieces. Wash the tomatoes. Cut the pineapple into small pieces. Trim the lemongrass, remove the outer hard leaves, wash the pale lower part and cut into small pieces.

2 Heat the oil in a wok or frying pan, stir in the curry paste and sear. Add the coconut milk and bring to a boil over high heat.

3 Add the lemongrass, sugar, fish sauce and lime juice. Add the chicken and pineapple and simmer uncovered for about 5 minutes.

4 Drop in the tomatoes and allow to heat thoroughly. Serve the chicken curry in small bowls with basmati rice.

Fried Chicken Breast
with Thai Sauce

Ingredients

For the meat:

4 boneless chicken breast portions
(about 5 ounces each)

2 tablespoons dark soy sauce

1 teaspoon crushed red pepper

1 tablespoon lime juice

$\frac{1}{2}$ teaspoon sugar · 1 garlic clove

4 tablespoons vegetable oil

salt · freshly ground red pepper

For the sauce:

2 garlic cloves · 1 red chili pepper

1 tablespoon sugar · 1 tablespoon

rice vinegar · 1 tablespoon lemon

juice · 2 tablespoons fish sauce

Preparation

SERVES 4

1 Rinse the chicken and pat dry. Mix the soy sauce, pepper, lime juice and sugar to make a marinade. Peel the garlic clove, crush with a press, and add to the sauce. Cover the meat with the marinade and allow to stand for at least 30 minutes.

2 For the Thai sauce, peel the garlic cloves and chop finely. Prepare the chili pepper, seed, rinse and chop finely. Mix the garlic and chili with 1 tablespoon boiling water, the sugar, rice vinegar, lemon juice and fish sauce in a small bowl.

3 Remove the chicken from the marinade and pat dry. Heat the oil in a pan and cook the chicken breasts for 8 minutes on each side until done. Season the chicken with salt and a little red pepper. Slice and serve with the Thai sauce.

Grilled Chicken Breast
with Wok Vegetables

Have you already woked today? One way of getting something good on your plates quickly is called stir-frying

Ingredients

4 boneless chicken breasts

1 teaspoon 5-spice seasoning powder

grated rind and juice of 1 lime

½ cup dark soy sauce

7 ounces sugar-snap peas

2 zucchini

2 medium carrots

2 tablespoons vegetable oil

¼ teaspoon chili powder

salt · ½ cup vegetable stock

3 ½ ounces sprouts
(e.g. soy bean or alfalfa)

2 tablespoons roasted sesame seeds

Preparation

SERVES 4

1 Rinse the chicken breasts and pat dry. Mix the 5-spice seasoning powder, lime juice and rind with 8 tablespoons soy sauce. Cover the meat with the marinade and allow to stand for 15 minutes.

2 Prepare and wash the sugar-snap peas and zucchini. Slice the zucchini. Peel the carrots and cut into thin strips.

3 Heat the oil in a hot wok. Sear the sugar-snap peas for 1 minute, stirring constantly. Add the zucchini and carrots and stir-fry for another 2 minutes. Season the vegetables with chili powder, 4 tablespoons soy sauce and salt. Add the stock and cook for another 5 minutes.

4 Fry the chicken breasts in a skillet on each side for about 3 minutes. Pour boiling hot water over the bean or alfalfa sprouts and allow to drain. Add to the vegetables with the sesame seeds. Cook for another 2 minutes, stirring constantly. Slice the meat and sprinkle with the remaining soy sauce. Arrange the vegetables on plates and serve with the meat.

Tip

Bean sprouts are easy to grow at home. All you need is moisture and warmth. Germinating equipment made of clay, glass or plastic is available in big home and garden stores.

Duck Breast
with Peanut Sauce

A heavenly dish for the connoisseur: Give your taste-buds a special treat and enjoy the best part of the duck with a nutty dip

Ingredients

1 ⅓ cups scented rice

3 boneless duck breasts

5 tablespoons vegetable oil

salt · freshly ground pepper

5 ounces salted peanuts

1 tablespoon red curry paste

¾ cup unsweetened coconut milk

¾ cup vegetable stock

3 tablespoons palm sugar (or brown sugar)

3 tablespoons rice vinegar

1 red and 1 yellow bell pepper

1 bunch scallions

2 garlic cloves

1 tablespoon fish sauce

Preparation

SERVES 4

1 Prepare the scented rice according to the instructions on the package. Reserve.

2 Rinse the duck breasts and pat dry. Heat 2 tablespoons oil in a large pan, put the duck breasts into the pan, skin side down, and fry for about 8 minutes over medium heat, then turn and fry for another 8 minutes. Season with salt and pepper, wrap in aluminum foil, place in the oven and keep warm at 175°F.

3 For the peanut sauce, crush the peanuts with a mortar and pestle. Heat 1 tablespoon oil in a pan and braise the curry paste for about 1 minute over low heat. Add the coconut milk and vegetable stock and boil for about 2 minutes. Add the peanuts, palm sugar, ½ teaspoon salt and rice vinegar and cook the sauce for about 10 minutes over low heat until thickened.

4 Prepare the bell peppers, seed, rinse and cut into strips. Prepare and wash the scallions. Cut the white section into thin rings, the green section lengthwise into strips. Peel the garlic cloves and chop finely.

5 Heat the remaining oil in the hot wok and braise the garlic until golden yellow. Add the vegetables and stir-fry for about 3 minutes. Season with the fish sauce.

6 Slice the duck breasts. Arrange the rice in bowls and serve with the sliced duck breast, vegetables and peanut sauce.

Sweet and Sour Duck
with Pineapple and Morels

Ingredients

1 pound boneless duck breast

5 dried Chinese morels · 3 garlic

cloves · 3 ½ ounces pineapple

1 ¾ ounces cucumber · 1 onion

2 scallions · 2 tomatoes · 3 table-

spoons vinegar · 4 tablespoons

honey · 1 tablespoon light or

½ tablespoon dark soy sauce

3 tablespoons fish sauce

2 tablespoons palm sugar

1 tablespoon tomato ketchup

2 teaspoons cornstarch · salt

4 tablespoons flour · freshly

ground pepper · 4-5 tablespoons

vegetable oil · a little cognac

Preparation

SERVES 4

1 Rinse the duck breasts, pat dry and remove the fat. Cut into bitesize pieces. Soak the morels for 20-30 minutes in tepid water. Drain and cut into strips.

2 Peel the garlic and crush with a mortar and pestle. Peel the pineapple and cucumber and cut into pieces. Peel and dice the onion. Prepare the scallions, wash and cut into small pieces. Cover the tomatoes with boiling hot water, peel, seed and dice finely.

3 Bring a little water to a boil with the vinegar, honey, soy sauce, fish sauce, sugar, tomato ketchup and garlic. Mix the cornstarch with a little cold water until smooth, then add to the pan. Bring to a boil briefly and season with salt.

4 Mix the flour with the salt and pepper and toss the duck in this mixture. Heat the oil and fry the duck, a few pieces at a time.

5 Add the pineapple, cucumber, tomatoes, onion, scallions and morels to the sauce and briefly bring to a boil. Season to taste with cognac and pour over the pieces of duck.

Breast of Duck
with Baked Bananas

Ingredients

2 large boneless duck breasts

(about 8 ounces each)

salt · freshly ground pepper

10 mini bananas · 2 eggs

1-2 tablespoons flour

1 1/4 cups flaked coconut

vegetable oil for frying

scant 1/2 cup mayonnaise

2 tablespoons curry powder

2-3 tablespoons unsweetened

coconut milk

1/2 tablespoon plum sauce · Chinese

seasoning (e.g. Dayong) · 1/2 bunch

each cilantro and Thai basil

Preparation
SERVES 4

1 Preheat the oven to 250°F. Rinse the duck, pat dry and score the skin with a knife forming diamonds. Season with salt and pepper.

2 Sear the skin side of the duck breasts in a skillet until crisp. Turn and sear the other side of the meat briefly, too. Roast the duck breasts for another 20 minutes on the middle rack of the oven.

3 Peel the bananas. Whisk the eggs. Toss the bananas first in the flour, then in the eggs, and finally in the flaked coconut. Press the coating on well. Heat the vegetable oil and fry the bananas in the oil until golden brown.

4 Stir the mayonnaise with the curry, coconut milk and plum sauce. Season to taste with salt, pepper and Chinese seasoning mix. Wash the herbs, pat dry and chop. Cut the duck breast into thin slices. Sprinkle with cilantro and basil and place next to the bananas. Serve with the dip.

Turkey Ragout
with Cilantro and Limes

Red Hot Chili Peppers: Red Hot Chili Peppers call the tune
here, too – Thai cuisine would not be the same without them

Ingredients

1 ¼ pounds boneless turkey
breast

2 red chili peppers

2 onions · 2 garlic cloves

1 ¼-inch piece fresh ginger
root

4 tablespoons vegetable oil

2 tablespoons fish sauce

2 tablespoons oyster sauce

2 tablespoons lime juice

1 teaspoon brown sugar

4 sprigs cilantro

1 lime

Preparation

SERVES 4

1 Rinse the turkey breast, pat dry and cut into bitesize pieces. Prepare the chili peppers, seed, rinse and cut into thin strips. Peel the onion and cut into thin segments. Peel the garlic cloves and ginger and dice very finely.

2 Heat the oil in a hot wok. Stir-fry the strips of chili pepper, onions, ginger and garlic briefly.

3 Add the strips of turkey and braise all together over high heat for about 3 minutes. Season the meat with fish sauce, oyster sauce, lime juice and sugar to taste.

4 Wash the cilantro and shake dry, pluck off the leaves. Scald the lime with hot water, rub dry and cut into segments. Serve the turkey ragout in bowls, sprinkle with cilantro leaves and garnish with segments of lime. Serve with scented rice.

Tip

Fish and oyster sauce are indispensable in Thai cuisine. Oyster sauce is dark brown and thickish, made from soy sauce and oyster extract. Fish sauce is made from anchovies, salt and water.

Turkey Meatballs
with Rice Noodles

It all goes round: Tiny meatballs become mouth-watering delicacies when made with exotic spices, mango and cilantro

Ingredients

1 pound boneless turkey breast

1 egg yolk

1 heaped tablespoon cornstarch

1 tablespoon fish sauce

1 teaspoon brown sugar

1 teaspoon curry powder

1 tablespoon paprika powder

1 chili pepper

3 1/2 ounces mango flesh

1 tablespoon chopped cilantro

freshly round pepper

8 stalks lemongrass

1 pound thin rice noodles

Preparation

SERVES 4

1 Rinse the turkey, pat dry and chop finely. Mix with egg yolk, cornstarch, fish sauce, sugar, curry and paprika powder. Preheat the oven to 400°F.

2 Prepare the chili peppers, seed, rinse and chop finely. Dice the mango finely.

3 Add the chili, mango and cilantro to the turkey mixture. Season with pepper. With moist hands, shape into small balls.

4 Wash the stalks of lemongrass and pat dry. Thread several balls onto the stalks and bake for about 10 minutes in the preheated oven, turning often.

5 Cook the noodles according to the instructions on the package. Pour off the water and allow to drain. Arrange on plates and serve with the skewered meatballs.

Tip

Alternately, have your butcher grind the turkey up for you. If you can't get lemongrass stalks, use wooden skewers instead, but soak these in water for at least 30 minutes before using.

Pork Stir-fry
with Bok Choy and Corncobs

*Green adds a little freshness: Bok choy, the Asian equivalent of
Swiss chard, isn't just a feast for the eyes, it also has a great aroma*

Ingredients

1 ⅓ cups scented rice

1 pound pork

2 garlic cloves

7 ounces carrots

7 ounces bok choy

7 ounces canned baby corncobs

3 tablespoons vegetable oil

3 tablespoons fish sauce

3 tablespoons oyster sauce

1 teaspoon brown sugar

Preparation

SERVES 4

1 Prepare the scented rice according to the instructions on the package. Reserve.

2 Rinse the pork, pat dry and cut into bitesize strips. Peel the garlic and chop into small pieces. Peel the carrots and slice diagonally.

3 Prepare the bok choy, wash and shake dry. Cut the stalks and leaves into strips crosswise. Allow the corncobs to drain in a sieve and trim the thick ends.

4 Heat the oil in a pan or a wok and briefly sear the garlic. Add the pork and stir-fry for about 2 minutes over high heat.

5 Add the carrots and corncobs and stir-fry for another 3 minutes. Then add the bok choy and braise for another 3 minutes, stirring constantly, until the vegetables are cooked but still firm to the bite.

6 Season to taste with fish sauce, oyster sauce and sugar. Serve the rice with the pork-vegetable mixture on plates or bowls.

Tip

In Thailand, as in other Asian countries, rice is a staple food. Thai scented rice, also known as aromatic jasmine rice, is a long-grain rice that develops a wonderful scent or aroma while cooking.

Egg Noodles
with Pork and Bok Choy

Ingredients

9 ounces Chinese egg noodles

10 ounces pork

2 garlic cloves

1-inch piece fresh ginger root

1 pound bok choy

3-4 tablespoons vegetable oil

5 tablespoons dark soy sauce

2 tablespoons oyster sauce

4 tablespoons lemon juice

salt

sugar

Preparation

SERVES 4

1 Cook the noodles according to the instructions on the package, then pour into a sieve and allow to drain well.

2 Rinse the pork, pat dry and cut into strips. Peel the garlic and ginger and chop finely. Mix the pork with the ginger and garlic. Prepare the bok choy, wash, shake dry and cut into wide strips.

3 Heat half the oil in a pan. Sear the pork over high heat for 3 minutes, then remove. Heat the remaining oil in the pan, add the bok choy and sear for 2-3 minutes, stirring constantly.

4 Add the noodles and meat, toss lightly and season to taste with soy sauce, oyster sauce, lemon juice, salt and sugar.

Spicy Pork
with Ginger

Ingredients

1 ½ pounds pork (without fat
and bone)

1 onion

1 dried chili pepper

1-inch piece of fresh ginger root

3 tablespoons vegetable oil

salt · freshly ground pepper

½ teaspoon each ground coriander,
turmeric and cumin seed

a little green from a scallion

1 tablespoon chopped parsley

Preparation

SERVES 4

1 Rinse the meat, pat dry and dice. Peel the
onions and dice finely. Prepare the chili pepper, rinse and chop finely. Peel the ginger and
either chop or grate.

2 Heat the oil and sear the meat well all round.
Season with salt and pepper. Add the ginger
and chili and braise for about 3 minutes.

3 Stir in the coriander, turmeric and cumin.
Add 1 cup water, cover and simmer for about
45 minutes.

4 Wash the scallion green, shake dry and cut into
rings diagonally. Sprinkle the pork with parsley
and scallion green, then serve.

Quick Beef
with Vegetables

Two-in-one: A stir-fry in the wok combines two different methods of cooking – quick frying and brief braising

Ingredients

for the meat:

1 red chili pepper

1 pound beef tenderloin

2 tablespoons cornstarch

freshly ground pepper

sugar

3 tablespoons soy sauce

2 garlic cloves

4 tablespoons vegetable oil

for the vegetables:

1 bunch scallions

9 ounces sweet potatoes

5 ounces sugar-snap peas

1 3/4 cups bamboo shoots (canned)

2 tablespoons vegetable oil

2 tablespoons rice wine

freshly ground pepper

1/2 cup chicken stock

Preparation

SERVES 4

1 Prepare the chili peppers, seed, rinse and chop finely. Rinse the beef, pat dry and cut into thin slices.

2 Stir the cornstarch with pepper, 1/2 teaspoon sugar, 1/4 cup water and the soy sauce until smooth. Peel the garlic, chop finely and add. Stir the marinade well, add the oil, chili pepper and meat, and mix everything together well.

3 For the vegetables, prepare the scallions, wash and cut into pieces. Peel the sweet potatoes, wash and slice thinly. Prepare the sugar-snap peas and wash. Pour the bamboo sprouts into a sieve, allow to drain and cut into strips.

4 Heat the oil in a hot wok. Remove the beef from the marinade, allow to drain and stir-fry quickly in the hot oil. Remove the meat. Gradually add the vegetables to the wok and stir-fry until tender but still firm to the bite.

5 Then add the meat to the wok again, add the marinade. Add the rice wine, pepper and chicken stock and stir everything together well. Bring to a boil and simmer for about another minute. Serve with basmati rice.

Tip

Try preparing this dish with Thai eggplant instead of sweet potatoes. If these should prove difficult to obtain, use local ones instead.

Beef and Vegetable Pot
with Egg Noodles

Thais do appreciate hearty fare, too: When beef and vegetables are cooked together, they make very good company

Ingredients

7 ounces Chinese egg noodles
(or spaghetti)

10 1/2 ounces beef (for stir-frying)

1 red chili pepper

3 garlic cloves

7 ounces canned baby corncobs

1 red bell pepper

1/2 bunch scallions

4 tablespoons vegetable oil

1 teaspoon mustard seeds

1/2 cup vegetable stock

3 tablespoons soy sauce

salt · freshly ground pepper

Preparation

SERVES 4

1 Cook the noodles according to the instructions on the package, drain, rinse with cold water and allow to drain again. Rinse the meat, pat dry and cut into thin, bitesize pieces.

2 Prepare the chili pepper, seed, rinse and cut into thin strips. Peel the garlic and slice. Allow the corncobs to drain in a sieve. Prepare the bell pepper, seed, rinse and cut into strips. Prepare the scallions, wash and cut into thin rings.

3 Heat the oil in a pan and braise the mustard seeds, garlic and chili. Add the bell pepper and meat. Reduce the heat and braise the bell pepper and the meat, but do not allow to brown. Add the vegetable stock and soy sauce, cover and allow to cook for 4 minutes over low heat. Add the corncobs and the scallions, cover and cook for another 4 minutes.

4 Finally stir in the noodles, re-heat, season to taste with salt and pepper, then serve.

Tip

Egg noodles are used a lot for soups and fried dishes in Thai cuisine. They are about as thin as spaghetti, which can be used as a substitute.

Thai Beef Tenderloin
with Green Asparagus

Ingredients

1 pound beef tenderloin

2 red chili peppers

1 1/2 teaspoons cornstarch

2-3 tablespoons soy sauce

2-3 tablespoons sherry

1 handful shiitake mushrooms

10 1/2 ounces green asparagus

9 ounces medium potatoes

1 small radicchio

2 tablespoons vegetable oil

2 tablespoons vegetable stock

freshly ground pepper

1/2 teaspoon sugar

Preparation

SERVES 4

1 Rinse the meat, pat dry, and cut into thin slices, across the muscle fibers. Prepare the chili peppers, seed, rinse and cut into small pieces. Dust the slices of meat with 1 teaspoon cornstarch, then sprinkle with 1 teaspoon each soy sauce and sherry, stir in the chili and allow to marinate in the fridge.

2 Prepare the mushrooms and chop up small if necessary. Wash the asparagus, peel the lower third, trim the ends. Cut the asparagus in half or in thirds. Wash the potatoes, halve and cut into thin slices. Separate the leaves of the radicchio, wash and pluck into pieces.

3 Heat the oil in a hot wok, add the meat and brown on all sides. Remove. Sear the asparagus and potatoes, stirring constantly. Add the mushrooms and braise, too, until the vegetables are tender but still firm to the bite.

4 Mix the remaining soy sauce, sherry and cornstarch with the vegetable stock, pepper and sugar, pour into the wok and bring to a boil briefly. Add the meat again and stir everything together over high heat. Finally stir in the radicchio and serve.

Fried Noodles
with Beef and Sprouts

Ingredients

9 ounces rice noodles

3 garlic cloves

2 red chili peppers

10 ounces beef

2 ounces garlic chives

1 $^1/_2$ ounces soy bean sprouts

2 tablespoons vegetable oil

1 $^1/_2$ ounces peas (frozen)

2 tablespoons fish sauce

2 tablespoons lemon juice

2 teaspoons brown sugar

a little scallion green

Preparation

SERVES 4

1 Cover the rice noodles in a bowl with boiling hot water and allow to swell for 10 minutes. Pour into a sieve and allow to drain. Reserve.

2 Peel the garlic and chop. Prepare the chili peppers, seed, rinse and chop. Rinse the beef, pat dry and slice thinly. Wash the garlic chives, dab dry and chop. Blanch the bean sprouts briefly, rinse with cold water and allow to drain.

3 Heat the oil in a hot wok. Add the garlic, chili pepper and beef and stir-fry for about 4 minutes. Add the noodles, cover and leave to braise for another minute.

4 Add the peas, fish sauce, lemon juice and sugar to the wok, stirring frequently, until everything is heated throughout. Add the bean sprouts and season to taste. Wash the scallion green, dab dry, cut into thin rings and add. Serve with lemon halves (optional).

Hot Beef Curry
with thin Egg Noodles

Harmonizing opposites: Fiery hot chili peppers and curry
paste are counterbalanced and soothed by mild coconut milk

Ingredients

1 pound beef tenderloin

2 stalks lemongrass

2 kaffir lime leaves

1 red chili pepper

1 teaspoon red curry paste

1 2/3 cups unsweetened
coconut milk

7 ounces thin egg noodles

2 sprigs cilantro

Preparation

SERVES 4

1 Rinse the meat, pat dry and cut into bitesize strips.

2 Remove the hard outer leaves from the lemongrass and cut the pale part of the stalks into pieces. Wash the lime leaves, pat dry and cut into very thin strips. Prepare the chili pepper, rinse and cut into thin rings.

3 Heat the curry paste with 2 tablespoons coconut milk in the hot wok, stirring constantly. Braise the meat in the curry paste for about 3 minutes. Add the remaining coconut milk. Add the lemongrass, lime leaves and chili rings and simmer for about 6 minutes over low heat.

4 Meanwhile cook the egg noodles in a generous amount of lightly boiling water according to the instructions on the package. Pour into a sieve and allow to drain. Wash the cilantro, shake dry and pluck off the leaves. Remove the lemongrass from the beef curry. Arrange the noodles on plates. Serve the beef over the noodles and garnish with cilantro leaves.

Tip

In this recipe, the chili pepper is not seeded, so the curry will be very hot since the heat is caused by the seeds. If you prefer it a little milder, seed the peppers first.

Index of recipes

Beef and Vegetable Pot 122
Beef Salad with Rice Noodles 34
Breast of Duck with Baked Bananas 111
Chicken Curry with Sugar-snap Peas 100
Chicken Satay with Peanut Sauce 12
Chicken Soup with Chilis 51
Chicken Soup with Galangal 50
Coconut Milk Soup with Shrimp 40
Crisp of Pikeperch with Black Sesame Seeds 80
Duck Breast Salad with Scallions 36
Duck Breast with Peanut Sauce 108
Egg Noodles with Pork 118
Fish Cakes with Ricotta Dip 89
Fish Fondue with Rice and Chili Sauce 72
Fish Patties with Herbs 88
Fish Soup with Noodles 48
Fried Chicken Breast with Thai Sauce 105
Fried Noodles with Beef 125
Fried Rice with Vegetables 62
Fried Shrimp Skewers with Chili Dip 96
Fried White Pomfret with Thai Shallots 84
Garlic Shrimp with Pineapple 90
Glass Noodle Salad with Cucumber 31
Grilled Chicken Breast with Wok Vegetables 106
Hot Beef Curry with thin Egg Noodles 126

Hot Cucumber Soup with Bell Peppers 57
Hot Thai Pickles with Mango and Papaya 58
Lemongrass Chicken on Rice Noodles 102
Lemongrass Soup with Shrimp 46
Mushroom-Vegetable Pan with Cauliflower 66
Ocean Perch with Vegetables 82
Papaya Shrimp Salad with Chili 28
Pork Stir-fry with Bok Choy 116
Quick Beef with Vegetables 120
Red Bream with Chili and Lemongrass 74
Red Chicken Curry with Cherry Tomatoes 104
Rice Noodle Salad with Duck 37
Rice Noodle Salad with Ground Meat 32
Rice Noodle Salad with Shrimp 26
Rice Noodle Soup with Chicken 42
Rice Noodles with Thai Basil 60
Rice Paper Packets with Shrimp 23
Rice Paper Rolls with Sweet and Sour Sauce 14
Rosefish Curry with Pineapple 76
Scallop Soup with Lemongrass 44
Seafood Ragout with Egg Noodles 86
Seafood Soup with Lemongrass 54
Shrimp and Pork Skewers with Chili Sauce 18
Shrimp Curry with Lemongrass 92

Shrimp Patties with Thai Chili Sauce 20
Shrimp Satay with Pineapple 24
Shrimp Soup with Mushrooms 45
Spicy Fillet of Salmon with Bok Choy 83
Spicy Pork with Ginger 119
Spring Rolls with Chicken 16
Squid Rings with Thai Basil 94
Sweet and Sour Duck with Pineapple and Morels 110
Thai Beef Tenderloin with Green Asparagus 124
Thai Vegetables in Rice Paper Wrappers 17
Turkey Meatballs with Rice Noodles 114
Turkey Ragout with Cilantro 112
Vegetable Ragout the Thai Way 64
Vegetable Rice in Banana Leaf 68
Vegetable Salad with Peanut Coconut Sauce 30
Vegetable Soup with Noodles 52
Vegetable Stir-Fry with Pineapple and Ginger 63
Wok Vegetables with Green Asparagus 67
Wok Vegetables with Squid 95
Wok-Fried Cod with Noodles and Vegetables 77
Wonton Soup with Spinach and Carrots 56
Wontons with Cod Filling 78
Wontons with Vegetable Filling 22

Copyright

Photo Credits

Cover photos: Susie Eising (front cover); Stock Food/Louise Lister (back cover)
W. Cimbal: 8, 9; StockFood/K. Arras: 67; StockFood/H. Bischof: 16; StockFood/M. Boyny: 31; StockFood/M. Brauner: 63; StockFood/G. Buntrock Ltd.: 37; StockFood/C. Carlott: 25; StockFood/S. Cato-Symonds: 21, 35, 125; StockFood/J. Cazals: 13; StockFood/R. Comet Photography: 30; StockFood/B. Danton: 88; StockFood/A. Deimling-Ostrinsky: 76; StockFood/T. DeSanto: 4–5; StockFood/Editon A. Zabert 7 (2nd from top left); StockFood/Susie Eising: 1, 10–11, 22, 27, 29, 36, 41, 43, 55, 61, 79, 85, 109, 110, 111; StockFood/S. & P. Eising: 2–3, 6 left, 7 center, 7 top right, 23, 47, 73; StockFood/Foodphotogr. Eising: 19, 38–39, 53, 59, 69, 81, 91, 93; StockFood/I. Garlick: 33, 75, 83, 87, 101, 123, 124, 127; StockFood/S. Irvine: 44; StockFood/Johansen: 45; StockFood/Kia Nu: 65, 98–99, 105, 115, 121; StockFood/C. Krüger: 50; StockFood/Louise Lister: 15, 49, 51, 97, 103, 113, 117; StockFood/D. Loftus: 118; StockFood/A. Mackevicius: 119; StockFood/S. Morris: 7 bottom left; StockFood/K. Newedel: 56, 57; StockFood/W. Pfisterer: 7 (2nd from bottom left); StockFood/Rosenfeld Images: 6 right; StockFood/Rynio: 62, 94; StockFood/M. Stock LTD: 7 top left; StockFood/Studio Bonisolli: 104; StockFood/W. Reavell: 17, 66, 89; StockFood/M. Urban: 82; StockFood/Westermann Studios GbR: 107; StockFood/F. Wieder: 70–71; 77, 95

Coconut Milk Soup (front cover): see recipe p. 40